BACK TO SQUARE ONE

Dedication

As a coach, my father did not spend much time laying down rules for his athletes about smoking, drinking, and keeping hours. At the beginning of the season he would simply say, "As far as training rules go, you can do whatever I do."

Though his players knew him as a superb teacher, and opposing coaches respected him as a brilliant gridiron tactician, it is the force of his own life and personal example that has made the deepest impact on those who have known him. When I meet men who played under him (his coaching career spanned more than forty years), I sense always that note of respect and affection that men reserve for another man whose influence has strengthened the fiber of discipline and integrity in their own lives.

It is with gratitude for the example his life has been to me and many other men that this book on practical Christian living is lovingly and respectfully dedicated to my father, ADE CHRISTENSON.

BACK TO SQUARE ONE

LARRY CHRISTENSON

Bethany Fellowship INC.
MINNEAPOLIS, MINNESOTA 55438

This material is also available in a cassette series by the same title.

All scripture references are taken from the Revised Standard Version of the Bible, unless otherwise indicated.

Published by Bethany Fellowship, Inc.
6820 Auto Club Road, Minneapolis, Minnesota 55438

Printed in the United States of America

Library of Congress Cataloging in Publication Data

Christenson, Laurence.
    Back to square one.

    1. Christian life—Lutheran authors. I. Title.
BV4501.2.C497   248'.48'41   79-16413
ISBN 0-87123-025-9

Preface

In one way the Christian life is like a game: You enter into an endeavor in which you are governed by a logic and a process which is built into the game. It is not normal in everyday life to smash into another person and knock him to the ground, but on a football field it is expected. One does not make ordinary, day-to-day decisions by twirling a dial or throwing dice, but in a table game like Monopoly it's the only way to move ahead. The Christian life is similar: A follower of Jesus is called to set aside the normal way things are done in the world and enter into a new kind of endeavor, a way of living, with a logic and process all its own.

In this book we use the image of a "game"—several games, in fact—to consider how a person can live the Christian life more effectively. There is something exciting and contagious about a game when one gets caught up in it. And the Christian life can have that same quality if a person is willing to enter into the logic and process which God has built into it.

Living the Christian life is like no other undertaking on earth. In other areas of endeavor, one can expect a growing sense of competence as knowledge is gained and applied. But the longer one lives the Christian life, the more clearly he recognizes how much beyond him and his own powers is the kind of life to which he is called.

Jesus said to His disciples, "Apart from me you can do nothing" (John 15:5). He did not say this to them at the beginning of their time together, the way a teacher might say to a new student, "To begin with I'll be right beside you, telling you exactly what to do." Jesus said these words in

His farewell discourse, after He had trained them for three years and was getting ready to return to His Father.

They did not absorb this startling truth all at once, nor do we. We don't pick up the logic and process of the Christian life at the first twirl of the dial, at the first toss of the dice! Learning to live in conscious dependence on Christ is a slow, often painful process. We have so much to unlearn of the world's way of thinking and doing. Again and again we have to go *back to Square 1* where we learn once more the truth that "in my flesh dwells no good thing" (Rom. 7:18 AV); and "who will deliver me from this body of death? Thanks be to God, *through Jesus Christ our Lord!*" (vv. 24, 25). Indeed, the whole Christian life might be described as one recurring reminder that "apart from me you can do nothing."

That is the logic which God has built into the Christian life, from beginning to end. That is the subject of this book.

Pentecost 1979   Larry Christenson

Table of Contents

V. THE STACK OF CARDS

VI. THE GOAL

I.

The Name of the Game

Every step forward in the Christian life
bears the marks of its origin.

Chapter 1

Back to Square One

Let me tell you about an intriguing idea that came to me one day. I had a picture in my mind of a game, a table game something like Monopoly.

Each player has a token. Everyone starts off on Square 1; but you can't move off Square 1 and go around the board until a little Red Bird comes along and sits down on Square 1 while you're there. Then you can go.

Watching the game progress, I saw the players move out and land on different places at the spin of a dial. Eventually the Red Bird settled next to me so I got off Square 1.

Going around the board, the players land on some squares where they have to pick up a card from the middle of the table. Every time I picked up one of those cards it said, "Go Back to Square 1." Then I had to sit and wait for the little Red Bird to come along again. It was rather frustrating.

I thought about that a bit, musing to myself, "Now this is a picture of the Christian life. The Holy Spirit's purpose for me is to get me back to Square 1. And that's His purpose for the church."

The key to the Christian life is getting back to Square 1 and continually moving out only from Square 1.

What is "Square 1"? That's the place where the individual can't do anything by himself. He has to wait for the little Red Bird to come along. We can spin the dial as much as we please, but it doesn't produce any lasting progress until that little Red Bird comes along to release us.

Think of the place where Christian life begins and this will make sense. To begin our life in Christ, we need salvation. We are forgiven and saved by the sheer grace of God, as we put our trust in Christ and His atoning death. We know that we can't "do" anything to gain salvation. God puts us on Square 1 and brings to a standstill every effort we've ever made toward our own salvation. We can't even begin to move until the Holy Spirit settles down next to us and releases us into life in Christ. That's salvation—or in theological terms, justification.

"By grace you have been saved through faith; and this is not your own doing, it is the gift of God—not because of works, lest any man should boast" (Eph. 2:8-9).

So now one is "saved," and the game of life is on! You spin the dial and take off, landing on some of those other squares along the way.

At first you don't realize it, but little by little it begins to dawn on you that the cards seem to be stacked against you. Every time you land on one of those squares that says, "Take a Card," the card reads, "Go back to Square 1." After this has happened two or three times, you might begin to get a little frustrated.

"Look at all those big important squares down the line, Lord: insights into scripture, charismatic gifts, holiness, Spirit-filled ministry, miracles, visions, Christian communities, winning souls for Jesus, making disciples of all nations! Why can't I move ahead to one of those? How in the world am I ever going to get around this board if I keep getting sent back to Square 1 all the time?"

When you ask that question, however you might phrase it, you're coming to grips with the real purpose of the game. *There is no moving ahead in the Christian life until we realize that we can't do it ourselves.* We cannot take over and run this life that's been given to us. Every step forward begins with a return to Square 1, where we receive a fresh release of the Holy Spirit.

Our imaginary game has five main features—
The Dial
The Token
The Playing Board
The Stack of Cards
The Goal

1. *The Dial*

The dial has a pointer that tells the player where to go on the next move. But it doesn't do any good to spin the dial until the little Red Bird comes along and lights on Square 1 while the player's token is there.

That's how progress in the Christian life gets under way. God brings to an end our ceaseless twirling of the dials of human activity—things we initiate and then piously ask God to bless. He sets us back on Square 1 where we learn to wait for the initiative of the Holy Spirit.

"In my flesh dwells no good thing" (Rom. 7:18, AV). I have no human knack, no power of my own to live the Christian life. Time and again I'm brought back to the place where I realize afresh that I cannot live this life out of my own resources. I have to be put back on Square 1 until it comes home to me in a new and vivid way that only the Holy Spirit can release me into this life.

Oh, I can spin the dial and go ahead, taking off on my own. But you know what that's like! How many projects have nosedived because we got nervous waiting for the Red Bird to come, and shot off on our own?

A woman told about her husband who had been converted and was all fired up to tell everyone about it. "We lost most of our friends that first year," she said. In the area of witnessing to our faith, we need to train our spiritual eyes to glance sidewards and see whether the Red Bird has settled down beside us. Otherwise our testimony may just turn people off.

This seems to be especially true with those closest to us, members of our own family or congregation. With them our testimony often must first be translated into the language of loving service. If a man is filled with the Spirit and the next Saturday morning his wife comes in to find him fixing the washing machine that's been on the blink for a month, or if gloomy Nellie has a deep experience with the Lord and her pastor walks by the church kitchen and sees her hanging up some bright, ruffly curtains around those dismal windows—there's a message about life in Christ coming across before a word is spoken.

The Holy Spirit may be quite ready to release us from Square 1 if we are pointed in the right direction physically, mentally and spiritually. But if our mind is locked in on some particular thing that is not on the Holy Spirit's agenda for us at this time, then we may have to cool our heels until we loosen up and become more sensitive to the Holy Spirit's initiatives.

Whatever the calling or ministry—be it witnessing, prayer, teaching, social action, giving—there is no fruitful work except that which is released by the Holy Spirit. The dial might point to a tremendous work which we think would build the kingdom of God. But if it is our own work done in our own way, we will be building with wood, hay and stubble. Though the work may be seemingly insignificant, when the little Red Bird comes along and releases us, it will be a building of gold, silver and precious stones— something that will endure (1 Cor. 3:11-15).

2. *The Token*

The token represents the player's progress around the board. The token cannot be moved any time or any place at a whim. The moves are given within the structure of the game.

The life in Christ is a *given* life from beginning to end. In regard to salvation we have to come to a clear-cut awareness that we can add nothing to that salvation. It is a gift; it is grace—all grace. *And the life that issues from that salvation is also of grace.* It depends completely upon the working of the Holy Spirit.

When God puts us back on Square 1, He's trying to

develop in us a grace-oriented mentality, an awareness that *we* can't do it, *God* must do it. This is what the Bible calls a *renewed mind.*

The desire to do things is a natural human tendency. And when we receive spiritual life we want to do spiritual things. But God says, "No, you can't do anything except that which the Holy Spirit empowers you to do." When He does, then real growth, true spiritual progress, can take place.

A deep yearning in many Christians is the desire to grow in the Spirit, to mature. The Bible urges us to "press on to maturity, not laying again a foundation of repentance from dead works and of faith toward God, with instruction about ablutions, the laying on of hands, the resurrection of the dead, and eternal judgment. And this we will do if God permits" (Heb. 6:1-3).

So often Christians are urged to activity with scarcely an afterthought given to the Spirit's participation. "Witness! Tithe! Obey! Love your wife! Get your family in order! Be concerned! Get involved! On to maturity! *Grow!*"

How different the Bible's call to maturity: "This we will do, *if God permits.*" While we urge one another to get our tokens moving down the board in a flurry of fleshly activity, God quietly sends us back to Square 1. There we realize, "I cannot love my wife just because someone urges me to do it. I must ask God to *permit* me to love my wife." This may sound strange but it is true. I cannot love my wife *as Christ loved the church* unless God releases me in the Holy Spirit to do it. My loving her is a work of God.

What we ought to be doing is earnestly urging *God:* "Lord, please *permit* me. Permit me to love my wife. Permit me to obey you. Let that little Red Bird settle down next to me here on Square 1. I know I can't do anything until He comes and releases me. Lord, permit it!"

Square 1 is where the Lord brings our self-effort to a standstill. That's what is meant by being a new creature in Christ—moving into life not under our own power but by

His gracious permission. "It is no longer I who live"—no longer I who love, no longer I who obey, no longer I who serve—"but *Christ who lives in me*; and the life I now live in the flesh I live by faith in the Son of God, who loved me and gave himself for me.

"I have been crucified with Christ" (Gal. 2:20).

All this is contrary to our natural mind. It's normal for us as human beings to think in terms of what *we* can or ought to do. It's all too easy—in fact, it's a continual temptation—to reduce the Christian life to a duty. "Come on! Get that token moving. Look at all those obligations out there waiting to be fulfilled!" Even if we get our thinking straight about salvation—that it's all by grace—we still think that living the Christian life is basically a duty. It's something *we* do in order to show God how thankful we are that He saved us.

God continually has to put us back on Square 1, where He brings home to us the beautiful truth that living the Christian life is a privilege which He graciously permits us to do. It is not by duty but by the grace of God that we move our tokens out onto the board and progress in the Christian life.

3. *The Playing Board*

As previously indicated, always having to wait for that Red Bird can be frustrating. It seems so restrictive. I can do only the things God lets me do. Look at all the opportunities, all the things out there that ought to be done! Why can't I be out there doing them? But God quietly insists, "Wait, the Red Bird hasn't come along. Stay on Square 1."

At first it *is* restrictive. God has to do that. He doesn't want us out there on the playing board relying on nothing but our own strength and our own resources. He wants every step taken to be by the initiative and in the power of the Holy Spirit. When He is able to get that through to us, whole new vistas of the playing board open up.

Looking at the Christian life as a duty is like wearing

blinders, oblivious to the tremendous possibilities that are open to those willing to enter into them only and always by the release of the Spirit.

When we get rid of the blinders, people around us sometimes get a little disturbed or annoyed or surprised; they see us entering into things that they didn't realize were on the playing board.

A man once told me about the experience of his five-year-old niece. She was in an evangelistic service with her mother. When the altar call was given she tugged at her mother's dress and said, "Mommie, can I go up?"

The mother answered, "You wait now, dear. In a few years you'll be able to do that. You're too young."

A little later came another tug at the dress. "Mommie, I want to go up and be saved."

"You wait a few years, dear. About the age of twelve that kind of thing happens."

"But I want to give my heart to Jesus."

The mother patted her on the head. Then the girl tugged one last time on the mother's dress. Looking down she saw tears streaming down the daughter's face. "Mama, Jesus just saved me."

Mama was going to hold her on Square 1 until the church, according to tradition, said it was all right for her to move. But the Holy Spirit doesn't always go along with our traditions. He sometimes releases us into things that stretch the traditions.

Something like that has been happening in the charismatic renewal. The "little children" have said, "Mama, can I have some of those gifts that I read about in the Bible?"

"Be quiet, dear. Those were for the early church. You don't need them. They were necessary only to get the church started."

But the little child keeps tugging away. "I really want those gifts, Mama. I'd like to pray for the sick. I'd even like to speak in tongues."

"Child, we just don't do that! It—it isn't our tradition!"

And then one day the little child comes home and reports, "Mommy, I got healed! Mama, I'm speaking in tongues!"

When the blinders of a duty-oriented religion begin to drop away, we catch sight of the tremendous potential of the Spirit. In one sense it is restrictive because we can't do a thing unless the Holy Spirit releases us into it. Yet at the same time it is liberating because the Spirit releases us into things we never dreamed of.

Here we ought to insert a word about *faith*. How do we know when the little Red Bird settles down on Square 1?

Is it because of a certain feeling? Not necessarily. Feelings are a natural and wonderful part of human life. But they are something like the keys of a piano: They are meant to be used in a variety of ways and combinations. You don't say, "E-flat is for classical music. Whenever I hear E-flat I know something classical is being played." You may come in some morning and find your kids using it to play chopsticks.

The coming of the Spirit may evoke a particular feeling, but a similar feeling can also be conjured up by other things. And sometimes the Spirit's coming may not be accompanied by any particular feeling; our feelings are not a reliable monitor of everything that is going on around us.

How then do you know when the Spirit comes? Do you take a promise out of the Bible? We sing that chorus, "Every Promise in the Book Is Mine." The Holy Spirit may indeed come in connection with a particular Bible promise. But we cannot casually pick up the Bible and randomly choose a promise simply on the basis of desire or hope.

Mary did not open the scroll containing the Book of Isaiah, read, "A virgin shall conceive and bear a son," and comment, "Now there's a wonderful promise. I'll claim that one for myself!" That promise came to her through the Lord's messenger. She was personally invited to step off Square 1, believing that word which was given. More than a word in her head, it was a faith quickened in her heart.

Faith is not a feeling. Nor is faith simply an idea in my head that I decide to accept. Faith is the living God entering into my innermost being. The Holy Spirit comes down and puts the living Christ in union with me and me with Him. To "step out in faith" means to step out in the confidence that Christ is with you.

Sometimes it can be a faltering step, one of fear and trembling. You wonder, "Did the Red Bird really come, or was it just my imagination?"

Faith is planted by the Holy Spirit at the deepest level of our being. Our feelings and ideas may not at once be aware of what has happened. The mind and emotions may even throw out counter-signals of uncertainty and doubt when one steps out in faith. It doesn't matter. In time they will learn that the plays in this game are being called by One higher and deeper than mere feelings and ideas: It is the living God himself who is the moving impulse behind the moves.

The impulse of the Holy Spirit, however, is not utterly mysterious. It has certain characteristic marks. Jesus said, "When the Spirit of truth [Holy Spirit] comes, he will glorify me" (John 16:14). If you believe the Red Bird is about to bring you into some particular thing, ask yourself, "Is God's glory at the center here? Is that my number-one concern?" And don't be afraid to probe your motives a little. Oftentimes under a veneer of concern for God's glory you find a solid chunk of old self-interest. A strong signal that you are moving in genuine faith is when concern for God's glory edges out self-interest.

Jesus also said to check out a plant by its *fruit* (Matt. 7:20). Will this new step bear good fruit? Will it build up the body of Christ? When the Holy Spirit calls us to take a step of faith, the fruit of faith will be produced.

4. *The Stack of Cards*

We began by referring to the stack of cards out in the

middle of the playing board. Every so often the player lands on a square that instructs him to take one of those cards. And every time it sends him back to Square 1.

From the outside the victorious Christian life may be characterized by joy and power. But that is only one side of the coin. Those looking on don't realize how often the card turns up saying, "Go back to Square 1." Time and time again God sends people back to that place of utter dependence upon Him, of waiting upon the Spirit.

A sainted old Bible teacher once said, "Everybody sees me teaching, people listening and crowding around afterwards; they think it's all up in the heavenly places. What they don't see is that when the meeting is over, I go home and die." What did he mean by that? He meant that to minister in the power of the Spirit, to be a channel of the gifts of the Spirit, in a profound sense is a crucifixion.

A priest made this keen observation about spiritual gifts: "The gifts are a humiliation because they take you beyond yourself to where God himself is at work. The gifts are a calling to service. The greater the gift, the less my life is my own."

To minister in the Spirit is to be moved by the Spirit out where we don't have anything to give and yet we must minister. Like Paul we are "in weakness and much fear and trembling," and yet the power of God is ministered through us.

To the onlooker, all that power and glory may look very marvelous and inviting. Remember Simon the Sorcerer's envious observation of Peter and Phillip's ministry (Acts 8:4-24)? But God knows what is really happening: He sovereignly keeps sending us back to Square 1 where we learn again to wait on Him. Possibly this may never show outwardly, but within God strips us down to the point where we have nothing and then He says, "Be released into what I want you to do."

And this brings another kind of frustration. At first we are frustrated because we are sent back to Square 1. But just about the time we come to accept that, along comes that little Red Bird and tells us to move out. One doesn't even get a chance to enjoy being a Square 1 martyr! When you feel strong you get shipped back to Square 1; and when you feel weak along comes the Red Bird.

It's this mixture of life and death that is hard. By nature we would choose to be completely one or the other—either miracle worker or martyr, but not both at the same time. To be set down on Square 1 when we're all fired up, and then to be released into ministry when we feel weak and helpless—that is the frustration and the glory of the Spirit-led life. "Always carrying in the body the death of Jesus, so that the life of Jesus may also be manifested in our bodies" (2 Cor. 4:10).

Do you see the issue in all this? Do you see the central question behind every move out there on the playing board? It is this: Who is going to be Lord? Who is sovereign in the church? Who has the right to determine the moves?

Most games simply state a set of rules. It's up to the player to determine the moves, just as long as one keeps within the rules. A lot of people look at the Christian life this way. As long as the Christian doesn't break the rules, he is free to call the shots.

But the Bible tells us it's a different kind of game. Jesus didn't leave His disciples a set of rules. He said, "When the Spirit of truth comes, *he* will guide you into all truth" (John 16:13).

We are *not* free to arrange our life any way we want to, just as long as we keep the rules. That's living under the law—a bondage from which Christ has set us free.

The freedom of the gospel is the freedom to move with the Spirit. It is the circumscribed liberty of knowing that until the little Red Bird comes along, nothing is possible for me; and when He does come, nothing is impossible.

5. *The Goal*

What have we learned about this game so far?

First of all we looked at the *dial*. The dial points out our next move. Who is going to determine the timing and direction of that move—the individual Christian or the Holy Spirit?

Then we looked at the *token*. It represents one's own progress around the board. We cannot move on to maturity by our own will and effort. We move only as the Holy Spirit graciously permits and empowers us to do so.

We saw that the *playing board* spreads out before us the possibilities of our life in Christ. Only the Holy Spirit can open up to us the full range and potential of that life.

The *stack of cards* in the middle of the board continually sends us back to the place we began. Again and again we must return to that place where we recognize our total dependency on the Spirit.

Now we conclude our overview by considering the *goal* of the game. What's the point of a game where the player keeps going back to Square 1?

Square 1 is the "Square of Remembrance." Martin Luther said, "We must continually remind people of the gospel, because they forget it." Though we may be able to recite it perfectly as a memorized doctrine, in the everyday affairs of life we too easily fall back to reliance on self. "O foolish Galatians! . . . Having begun with the Spirit, are you now ending with the flesh?" (Gal. 3:1, 3).

When God puts me back on Square 1 my flesh cries out, "I'm not getting anywhere!" And that's just the point— that's the point of the whole game. We can move forward in the Spirit only as our flesh dies. One man put it beautifully this way: "Christian growth refers to the growth of the Spirit's work in our lives. The Spirit grows and moves forward. We die and move backwards. Christ lives, we die. That's Christian growth."

"The Spirit grows and moves forward. We die and move backward . . . "—back to Square 1.

The Lord doesn't put us there to do the same work in us over and over. He puts us there as a reminder that every step forward in the Christian life bears the marks of its origin. "As therefore you received Christ Jesus the Lord, so live in him" (Col. 2:6). How did you receive Christ Jesus? By giving up reliance on yourself and relying on Christ. How are you going to live in Him? The same way.

So the goal of the game is not to grow and become something in ourselves, but continually to return to the place where Christ can become something in us. Luther put it this way: "Progress in the Christian life is losing all that is our own and starting anew again and again."

The Spirit is continually opening up new sections of the playing board, new dimensions of our life in Christ. Each experience is unique. The experience of repentance is not the same as the experience of prophesying; interpreting a vision is not the same as tithing; meditation is not the same as works of mercy. But every experience, no matter how different, and no matter how far along the road of Christian maturity, starts from the same place—Square 1, the place of dependence upon the Spirit.

When the Lord sends us back to Square 1 we can be certain He's planning the next step forward in our Christian walk!

II.

The Dial

There is no fruitful work
except that which is released by the Holy Spirit.

Chapter 2

All Things New

"Behold, I make all things new" (Rev. 21:5).

There is a difference between making all new things and making all things new. When one makes all new things, the old is set aside and one starts over from scratch. But if one makes all things new the old is refashioned, reshaped, realigned, reformed, restored—made new.

That's what God does. He is not an annihilator; He is a redeemer. He does not obliterate the old; He renews it. He does not make all new things; He makes *all things new.*

When God came walking in the Garden of Eden in the cool of the day and found Adam and Eve awkwardly draped with fig leaves, He did not turn away in disgust and say, "I will make a new thing."

When the earth had corrupted itself in the days of Noah, God did not smash the planet into oblivion and say, "I will make a new thing."

When the people of Israel melted down their golden earrings and bracelets and fine vessels to fashion a golden calf which they could worship, God held back His wrath; He did not utterly destroy the people He had chosen and turn away, saying, "I will make a new thing."

When a star came to rest over Bethlehem and shed its light down upon a world of men who willfully walked in darkness rather than light, God did not abandon them to that darkness and say, "I will make a new thing."

When those men who followed Jesus during the years of

His ministry, and were called to be apostles, fell away in the hour of His suffering and humiliation, denying Him and fleeing, God did not overrule Christ's call of these men and say, "It's all done with them; I will make a new thing."

When the Holy Spirit, who grafts men into the body of Christ and grieves with an awesome, holy, and divine grief because men walk careless of the calling to which they have been called, making light of the covenant into which they were baptized, God does not give up on them and say, "I will make a new thing."

When the church of the born again, over and over through the centuries, has grown complacent and corrupt and careless of her calling, God has not rejected her and said, "She is beyond all hope; I will make a new thing."

If God's way of starting something new were to sweep away everything that is old and broken and worthless and make all new things, our whole race and this world would have perished long ago. But God has chosen another way. He has chosen to make all things new. He has chosen to enter into this old, broken, worthless world and renew it by His presence. Renewal is what happens when God intervenes in our human situation. Renewal is "Immanuel," God-with-us; renewal is *incarnation*.

The incarnation is God's great paradigm, God's model, for initiating something new. When God became man He let it be known once and for all that He was not going to make all new things, He was going to make all things new. He was going to let His Son enter into every broken, diseased, sin-blackened situation in this world, change it, and make it new.

The secret of a new beginning is not to sweep away all that we assume is old and weak and ineffective, building according to some newer or better model—whether that be dictated by theology, liturgy, social action, or whatever. The secret is not in any of these things that we might choose to do. The secret is the intervention of God. "Behold, *I* make all things new!"

If we want to see genuine renewal, then the first thing we must do, the fundamental thing we must do, is *expect the intervention of God.* Until God intervenes, we will have a good program, nothing more. When God intervenes we have renewal.

This sense of expectancy does not function automatically. It is possible to have false expectancy or misguided expectancy, or superficial and inadequate expectancy. We may be expecting God to intervene in the wrong place, or failing to expect His intervention where we ought to. Our expectancy needs to be refined and sifted so that it coincides more and more perfectly with God's plan for renewing His church.

The paradigm or model of renewal is the incarnation. The life of Jesus Christ upon the earth is the master act of divine intervention. When God makes something new it is going to bear the marks of the incarnation upon it. For God's whole plan centers in Jesus and flows forth from Him. He is "the pioneer and perfecter of our faith" (Heb. 12:2). He has blazed a trail before us and He himself will bring us to the end of that trail.

Seven marks of the incarnation can help us focus our expectations in the places where God is waiting to intervene and make all things new.

1. *The Mark of the Stable*

Jesus was born in a stable. This is where God initiated His renewing work. It was not the choice of Mary or Joseph that Jesus should be born in Bethlehem—certainly not in a cow barn. It was God's choice. The renewing work began in the place and in the way determined by God.

Look for this in what the Spirit initiates: The mark of the stable. Does this prayer group, this conference, this program of social action, this change in a person's life bear the mark of *God's initiative?* Has God set this thing in motion or are we off and running, doing our own thing, piously hoping that God will tag along and bless it?

The key word here is *initiative*. One of the greatest obstacles to God's purposes is the multitude of activities that don't have the mark of the stable upon them. They are good works but they are not God-initiated works.

This problem is especially acute in the area of social action; we face here such a bewildering variety of needs. Every morning when we wake up there are a thousand concerns within walking distance of our front doorsteps. Which one or two or three can we become involved with in the time which is available to us? And precisely *how* should we become involved? What kind of help or action will be effective?

A man once told us about a family in desperate straits, who had come to their congregation for help. The congregation began to pull together some resources to help them out. But then a word of prophecy came, "Don't give hamburger to those I have put on husks."

God put the Prodigal Son on husks in order that he would come to himself and return to his father's house. If someone had come to him with regular meals, he might have stayed in the pig sty forever. God was dealing with this family in a similar way. If the congregation had simply gone ahead with its own plans, God might never have accomplished His purpose. They had to let God intervene and set the direction.

A stable is not the most likely place for a king to be born. It violates human sensibilities and common sense. But God knew what He was doing. It was the right place and the right way to begin His work of renewal.

Expect God to intervene. Expect Him to put the mark of the stable on whatever He wants you to be involved in. Expect Him to reveal how and where and when He wants to get a renewing work under way.

2. *The Mark of the Carpenter Shop*

Jesus grew up working in Joseph's carpenter shop. We know almost nothing about those years except for a brief glimpse when He was twelve years old. For thirty years He was there—thirty years of quiet growth and development, of quite ordinary daily life; not dramatic, not spectacular; hardly worth writing about. Yet it was an indispensable part of the renewing work God was doing through Jesus.

Look for this in the things God initiates: The mark of the carpenter shop. Does this work exhibit a quiet growth and stability in everyday situations? Do these people know how to endure the ordinary? Have they learned to be faithful in the routine of little things?

The key word here is *ordinary*. "Behold, I make *all* things new!" Not just the big things, not just "spiritual" things—*all* things. Ordinary things; everyday things; dull, boring things; unpleasant things. One of the characteristics of people being renewed by God is that they experience the intervention of God in the most ordinary situations.

Agnes Sanford said that after a renewing work in her life she discovered she could prepare the evening meal in half an hour, whereas before it had always taken her three times that long. God, intervening in a thoroughly practical way, gave a busy housewife an extra hour of time every day. Expect God to do that. He wants to put the mark of the carpenter shop on the things He sets in motion.

The carpenter shop offers a hundred opportunities a day to expect the intervention of God. You go to answer the phone; even before you pick up the receiver you pray that God will put himself into the conversation. You head for a committee meeting which has every prospect of turning into an unpleasant confrontation and consciously you plan on the intervention of God. You may have prepared thoroughly for the meeting. But the preparation is not what you put your ultimate trust in. The difference will be in whether or not God intervenes in that situation. Perhaps He will use what you have prepared, but perhaps not. "The plans of the mind belong to man, but the answer of the tongue is from the Lord. A man's mind plans his way, but the Lord directs his steps" (Prov. 16:1, 9). Make your plans, work and prepare, but expect some surprises.

The intervention of God is not simply a divine benediction on what you are doing. It is the active involvement of God. It causes something to happen that wouldn't otherwise happen.

I like to call this the X-factor. You lay out the equation

and put into it everything you know about the situation—

Peter + long robe and sandals — boat = sink.

That is the human equation. But Peter stepped out in faith and added the X-factor—

Peter + long robe and sandals — boat + THE INTERVENTION OF GOD = WALK!

The intervention of God brings about a new result, something that wouldn't otherwise happen. And the point of using Peter for our illustration is this: It doesn't happen automatically. It requires expectation. When Peter began to doubt, he moved back into the human equation and sank.

The quality of our everyday life can be completely renewed when we begin to add the X-factor. We have found, for instance, that in disciplining children the X-factor makes all the difference. As a father I can spank a disobedient child and it will do some good in controlling his outward behavior. But there is no guarantee that a spanking will change the inner attitude of the child, no guarantee that he will repent and come to a change of heart. That requires the intervention of the Holy Spirit. And for this I must exercise faith. I must say, "Lord, I can discipline my child the way your Word tells me to do, but only you can touch his heart. I can do the outward thing—the spanking—but unless you step in and use this occasion, nothing will happen on the inside."

Expect God to intervene. Expect Him to put the mark of the carpenter shop on you. Expect Him to intervene in the ordinary matters of everyday life.

3. *The Mark of Jordan*

At the river Jordan the Holy Spirit descended and remained upon Jesus. He was anointed with power for His ministry.

Look for the mark of Jordan in true renewal. Does this person or this community or this congregation have the anointing of the Holy Spirit for the ministry they are performing?

The key word here is *anointing*. There is a lot of man-appointed and tradition-appointed and self-appointed ministry going on today. This is not the kind of ministry that makes all things new. Unless a ministry is appointed by God and anointed with the Holy Spirit, it has no power to renew.

Does this mean that masses of people engaged in Christian work, clergy and laity, should head for the showers and turn in their uniforms? Should we wait for God to raise up truly "spiritual" ministry?

The vast majority of people who are engaged in Christian work are there because at some point in their life they responded to a genuine call of God. But some of them, somewhere along the line, have become discouraged or bored or weary or disillusioned. They need a fresh anointing of the Holy Spirit. They need a baptism of power. They need the assurance that when they move out to minister, they will move under the anointing of the Spirit.

Here is a place where we need to pray not only for ourselves but for others. "Lord, intervene! Anoint this pastor, this priest, this prayer group leader, this prophet, evangelist, teacher! Put the mark of Jordan on them!"

One of the greatest joys I have as a pastor is to see my people move into anointed ministry. Once I was at the altar together with a layman whom we had just recently called to share in the personal ministry service that we have once a month. As two people came forward for prayer, he received a very clear word for them. As I started praying for them, he suddenly realized that it was the same word which he had received. The people we were praying for were greatly encouraged when he shared it. But it was even more of an encouragement to him. He had been a little uncertain about entering into this kind of ministry. But several other men had discussed it, prayed about it, and felt that it was right. And as he stepped out in faith, the anointing began to come.

God wants anointed ministry within the body of Christ.

Expect Him to intervene. Expect Him to put the mark of Jordan on those who have a call to ministry. Expect His anointing for a Spirit-powered ministry.

4. *The Mark of the Wilderness*

Immediately after He was anointed for ministry, Jesus was led by the Spirit into the wilderness to be tested by the devil. This was not an interruption in God's plans for making all things new through Jesus. The Spirit led Him. It was a necessary encounter in Jesus' life.

Look for this when the Spirit initiates something new: The mark of the wilderness. Have we faced up to temptation and testing? Have we been out there in the wilderness where God seems to have become silent and the devil speaks loud and clear?

The devil demonstrated his basic tactic in the Garden of Eden and he hasn't changed it since. He introduces into your mind a doubt of God's Word and of God's call upon your life. He questioned Eve: *Did* God say you shall not eat of the tree? Maybe you misunderstood Him. Maybe it doesn't apply in the unusual situation you now face. Is it reasonable for you to go on living in this childish dependency? If you eat, you will become like God. . . .

Jesus had just come from the Jordan where the voice from heaven spoke, "You are my beloved Son, in whom I am well pleased." It was His messianic call. And the devil's first word was, "*If* you are the Son of God, turn these stones into bread. . . ."

No matter how subtle or varied the devil's attacks may be, behind them you will always find the same basic thrust: (1) God's Word doesn't count here; you can set it aside. (2) The call you thought God had put upon your life is no longer certain; you had better consider some other options.

In the wilderness, God intervenes in a special way. Not usually through circumstances or miracles, nor visions and revelations, but through His naked Word. The key word here is *remember*. When the devil has you in the wilderness, you must remember the word God has already made known to you—the Scriptures, to begin with. And the call He has put upon your life, the ministry He has committed to you.

The wilderness serves a special purpose in any work of renewal. God uses it to show us potential weaknesses in our own character or particular danger areas in the kind of ministry or calling He has given us. He doesn't merely tell us about these; He shows us. He lets the devil probe us until we recognize the fact that we are indeed up against a spiritual foe with awesome power at his disposal. Then it is that we must remember God's word to us and trust the truth and authority of that word against every doubt.

Have you ever wondered why pressures and tensions and misunderstandings can thrive in a Christian fellowship, while at the Rotary Club or the Women's Club people seem to get along fine? Is it because Christians, for all their talk, really are hypocrites after all, while those who follow only the golden rule actually practice what they preach? There is more here than meets the eye. When Christian people begin to take real fellowship and community seriously, they become a threat to the devil in a way that a secular organization never does. From the moment Christians begin even talking seriously about their life together as believers, they go down on the devil's agenda for a trip through the wilderness.

When people move toward some form of Christian community, you can usually tell where they are in relation to the wilderness just by asking, "How's it going with your community?" If they are bubbling over with enthusiasm, they haven't gotten to the wilderness yet. If they're shifty-eyed, like a man looking for the closest exit, they are probably in the wilderness. If they half shrug their shoulders, and smile, and their manner is something you might describe as peaceful and unthreatened, chances are they've had a turn or two in the wilderness and come through it. They saw a lot of selfishness and thoughtlessness exposed in themselves and in others but they also learned that God's Word can knit people together despite all that.

Expect God to intervene. Expect Him to put the mark of the wilderness on us and on our fellowships. Expect Him to put us to the test so that we will be prepared for our calling.

5. *The Mark of the Synagogue*

It was Jesus' custom each Sabbath Day, the Gospels tell us, to go to the synagogue. The word "synagogue" means a place for coming together. Jesus came together with the people of God. He shared in their worship and life.

When the Spirit initiates a work, the mark of the synagogue will be present. Do we faithfully share in the life and worship of God's people? Not just our prayer communities and close friends, but all of God's people? Jesus did not isolate himself with just His disciples and those who believed in Him. He went to the synagogue, which meant that He identified himself with the whole people of God. Do we feel that sense of identification with the whole church of God?

The key word here is *come together*. God does not intervene in a vacuum. When an individual or a group is experiencing a renewing work of God, there is a special obligation to come together with fellow Christians for the normal occasions of worship and shared activity. God's renewing work embraces the whole church. "Behold, I make *all things* new."

Two attitudes toward the church among spiritually awakened people undermine God's purposes. One is *separatism*. Separate yourself from all those worldly church people, cozy-in with your own group of "spiritual" people and forget about everyone else. The tendency is always present in a time of awakening. A hurry-up spirit takes over and the patient work of relating to *all* of God's people is shunted aside.

In 1963 my wife and I attended a conference in Germany. Our congregation had begun to move into charismatic renewal a year or two earlier. We were still new and, to a large degree untried, in these new experiences. At this conference we met some other Lutherans who had quietly experienced these things many years earlier. They were an encouragement to us, for we saw in them maturity and depth. One of the things they told us was this: "Stay in the church. If they push you out the front door, come in the back door; if they throw you out the back door, come around the front again."

At the synagogue in Nazareth they tried to throw Jesus down a cliff. He was back for services the next Saturday. He didn't separate himself.

The other attitude toward the church which undermines God's purposes is a *militant proselytism*. "You're a lukewarm, carnal Christian and I've got the very thing you need. Just step over here into the prayer room where we can minister to you and you'll be fine"—admittedly a caricature of renewal, but this is the kind of impression that some people carry away. When renewed individuals size up the local parish the way Crazy Horse sized up Custer—as so many scalps to be had—the very ones we want to help shy away.

When renewal comes a person often has something wonderful to share with his fellow Christians. But that someone also has many things to *learn*. Coming together in the local fellowship is a two-way street. One must be ready to listen as well as to speak; ready to work as well as to pray and study. This is what earns a sympathetic hearing for the renewal message. This is what opens the door for God to intervene and let renewal spread like a good infection.

We have had people finally open up to charismatic renewal in our congregation after living side by side with it for ten years. That quiet, unspectacular coming together bore its fruit in God's good time.

Expect God to intervene. Expect Him to put the mark of the synagogue on a work of renewal. Let God's people come together—all of God's people—so He can make them new.

6. *The Mark of the Cross*

Here Jesus died. Here the glad sounds of rejoicing fall silent. We stand in the presence of the mystery that the renewal of God must pass through the valley of suffering and death.

Look for the mark of the Cross in renewal. Does this person or group know what it means to die to self? Has self-interest, ambition, pride, ego experienced crucifixion?

The key word here is *self*. The Cross deals with our self-life. The Cross deals with that stubborn determination to have my own way, do my own thing, direct my own life.

The self is a tough old codger. It is an enemy of God's purposes because it insists on its own way. "All we like sheep have gone astray; we have turned every one to his own way" (Isa. 53:6).

If we want to see renewal, we must expect God to intervene and deal decisively with the self-life. We must look for Him to supply the situation which will work death to the ideas and plans and habits of life which stem from our own will. And when He does, we must do as Jesus did: quietly accept it.

A friend of ours had served in the ministry for nearly twenty-five years. He was respected by his fellow clergy. He had held responsible posts in the denominational structure. Then he got involved in the charismatic movement.

"All at once," he said, "my testimony became suspect. Other clergy wouldn't believe it when I told them it was renewing the life of my parish. I was treated like a liar."

I asked him whether he was any longer considered to serve on official boards or committees. He laughed good naturedly, "I couldn't get elected dog catcher!"

He accepted it gracefully. But I knew that to be so regarded by his fellow clergy was a death.

Expect it. Expect God to put the mark of the Cross on many areas of our lives, things we may have looked upon as harmless or inconsequential but things He knows to be little hidden fortresses of the self-life and therefore enemies of His renewing work.

7. *The Mark of the Open Tomb*

Jesus rose from the dead. This is the very heart of God's work of renewal. It is the ultimate illustration that renewal is beyond man; it is the work of God.

Up from the tomb God brought forth a new life which was itself life-begetting. "The Father has granted the Son to have life in himself . . . [and] the Son gives life to whom he will" (John 5:26, 21).

Look for this in those things the Spirit initiates: The mark of the open tomb. What happens when people get next to renewed people? Do they change? Does something really happen?

The key word here is not just fresh ideas and new experiences, but new life in Christ. That's the heart of renewal.

You don't have to agree with a man's politics or cheer for the same ball club he does in order to catch the measles from him. Just stick around him for a while and you'll catch it. If some spiritual experience has quickened in us the life of Jesus, then we should expect God to infect those around us with that same life.

We may never get everybody in the church around to agreeing on a theology of spiritual experience—and even if we did the Holy Spirit would probably blue-pencil half of it. (That doesn't mean that we should not take seriously the theological task.) What we *can* do, however, is share the life that the Spirit has given us.

God's plan for renewal is bigger than any experience or any movement. It takes in all the church and, ultimately, all of creation. It is the result of a sovereign initiative of God, who looks out over the playing board of our life, surveys all our broken hopes and says, "Behold, I make all things new!"

Chapter 3

The 5-W Question

"Beware of false prophets, who come to you in sheep's clothing but inwardly are ravenous wolves. You will know them by their fruits" (Matt. 7:15-16).

Have you ever talked yourself into starting something about which you weren't quite convinced and then afterwards wished you hadn't? Have you ever gone into something with which you didn't feel comfortable, only to regret it afterwards? Most of us can think of times in our lives when we decided to do something that bore bad or bitter fruit.

How can we avoid getting into those kinds of situations? What can we do to bear good fruit? Jesus has an answer. It's a simple answer, though not simplistic. It takes careful thought to understand and apply Jesus' words. But when we do discover this answer, we will find that Jesus has made practical provision for good fruit to come forth in our lives.

In Matthew 7:15-20, Jesus reveals to us His mind on this matter. He begins by saying, "Beware of false prophets." The positive side of that would be "Look for true prophets."

True and False Prophets

What is a prophet? He is a spokesman for God. A prophet is someone who brings God's right-on word to people in a specific situation. Prophets have been important in the whole history of God's dealings with His people. In the Old Testament we have the whole stream of prophets from Samuel to Malachi. In the New Testament the church is "built on the foundation of the apostles and prophets."

Jesus said to beware of prophets who bring a word which they claim is from God but that really isn't from God. One recalls the story of the prophet Micaiah in the time of Ahab. A whole band of prophets came and prophesied exactly what the king wanted to hear. King Jehoshaphat from Judah was sitting by and grew suspicious. It sounded too pat.

"Isn't there another prophet?" he asked.

Ahab answered, "There is another prophet, but he never prophesies good things about me."

Jehoshaphat prevailed and they sent for Micaiah who came and let it be known that a lying spirit was in the mouths of the other prophets. Ahab resented Micaiah's word and had him put him in prison, but his word proved true.

A true prophet is one who speaks the word of the Lord regardless of consequences. The false prophet claims to speak the word of the Lord but doesn't. He's like the prophets in Jeremiah's day who said, "Peace, peace," but there was no peace.

The outward appearance of a false prophet may be quite like that of a true prophet. The words they come with may sound good. But they don't produce good results. Jesus said that inside they're like ravenous wolves. They're disguised like sheep but actually they are wolves who will eat you up. They don't come to build; they come to destroy.

Jesus goes on to say that you don't gather grapes from thornbushes or figs from thistles. A thornbush in Israel, the buckthorn, has little berries which look very much like grapes. There is also a thistle that has a flower which looks very much like a fig from a distance. But when one sees it up close, he finds out that it isn't the real thing. It has only the outward appearance of the real thing.

Jesus said false prophets will be exposed by the fruit they produce. So the crucial question is: Does the word they bring produce good fruit or bad fruit?

Who are the false prophets today? At the conclusion of this teaching Jesus says, "Everyone who *hears* these words of mine and *does* them will be like a wise man." *Hearing* plus *doing* equals *obedience*. Set against that truth, a false prophet is any person that waters down our obedience to the words of Jesus.

False Prophets Today

Look carefully at this word of Jesus. Jesus does not say, "Everyone who obeys *me*." He says, "Everyone who obeys *my words*."

How much does a little child know about the mind of his father? Not very much. Only the few things his father has told him. He can't say, "I think I know my dad and, even though he said to do this, I'm going to do something else because I know my dad."

"Who has known the mind of the Lord, or who has been his counselor?" (Rom. 11:34).

The false prophets in our day say that you don't have to worry about the explicit word or commandment that Jesus spoke. We can take a much broader view of His universal love and compassion and grace. And in saying this they set aside the specific words that He spoke, words about obedience, purity, faithfulness. That kind of prophet brings forth bad fruit. He sets aside the clear commandments of Jesus in the name of some "higher understanding"; but Jesus said, "Obey *my words*." There are many false-prophet voices today that are trying to set aside the hard commandments of Jesus, water down our obedience to Jesus in the name of "love."

William Barclay in his commentary on these verses says, "It's the old story that goes all the way back to New Testament times when they said, 'God has forgiven us all our sins in Christ, isn't that right? Yes, that's right. Well then, God will forgive and, after all, our sin is simply giving God's wonderful grace an opportunity to operate.' They even said, 'Let us sin all the more that grace may abound.' " But Barclay goes on to say that any teaching that takes the steel out of character, any teaching that takes the Cross out of Christianity, any teaching which eliminates the threat from Christ's voice, any teaching which pushes judgment into the background and makes us think lightly of sin, that is false teaching.

Facing the False Prophet Within

This brings us right down to the debates that we suggested at the beginning, the debates that go on within our own heart between the words of Jesus and the words of false prophecy. We've all had them. St. Paul says, "With my mind I serve the law of Christ, but I see another law in my members at war with the law of my mind making me captive to the law of sin and death" (Rom. 7:22-23).

There is a struggle going on within us, a struggle between the words of Jesus and the words of false prophecy that would water down our obedience to Christ. Our feelings easily identify with those words of false prophecy that offer some pleasantness in the immediate situation, while the word of Christ seems hard. This is where the battle is joined: What are we going to base our decision upon, the words of Jesus or the words that would water down obedience to Jesus? How we answer will determine the kind of fruit we bring forth.

When I consider only my own feelings, I can see all kinds of potential for evil. Does that mean that I have no hope but to bring forth evil fruit? No, it doesn't. Because the kind of fruit that comes forth in my life is going to be determined by what word I *act* upon. When I look within myself I'm looking for a word that God has planted there, a word I can act upon in obedience to Jesus. That brings forth good fruit.

If I look simply at my own potential, the flesh is always there, with its tendency toward the easy way. The old sinful nature would like to rear its ugly head, but by God's grace it can be kept in the place of death, it can remain on the Cross. As I choose, decision by decision, to obey Christ, good fruit comes forth.

Every morning when I wake up I can glance within and thank God for the word He has put within me to bear fruit for that day. The wise man is one who builds his life upon obedience to the words of Jesus, and thereby brings forth the fruit of righteousness.

The 5-W Question

Let me warn you about a particular strategy of the devil. You're battling temptation to disobey a word from God, and the thought comes, "I don't really want to obey. I know I should but I don't want to. Therefore it is hypocritical for me to do it." The devil chimes right in and says, "Yes, go along with the word that will make your action more in keeping with the way you really feel, so that you can be your own person and be honest about it."

Well, now, where did that *first* thought come from, the thought that Jesus is calling you to something higher, something better? Isn't that a part of you, too? Yes, that is a part of you ever since you have been united with Christ. That desire for something higher and better, that desire to obey Jesus, is as much a part of you as the fleshly temptation to rebel against the ways of God. The desire to follow Jesus is *you*, even though it may not touch your feelings as powerfully as the rebellion.

So your choice is, "Which part of me am I going to follow? *Which word within will win?*" (That's the 5-W question!) Your answer to that question tells you the kind of fruit you are going to bring forth.

Which word within will win, the word of Jesus or the word of the flesh? That word of Jesus is part of you, and is much stronger than any words that the devil might whisper in your ear. "It is no longer I who live, but Christ who lives in me" (Gal. 2:20). When the desire to make a decision that honors Christ springs up in your heart, you can say, "That's me and that's the word that's going to win! That's the word I identify with." As you do identify with that word, as you say "Yes" to that word, good fruit will come forth.

The word of Jesus that comes into your heart is the raw material for a life that releases the same kind of fruitfulness that Jesus brought forth. It is not something that you do; it is something that you allow Jesus to release within you as you say 'yes' to His word. The words are within you—the words of Jesus and the words of the false prophets. The question is simply: *Which word within will win?*

III.

The Token

Living the Christian life is a privilege which God graciously permits us to do. It is not by duty but by the grace of God that we move our tokens out onto the board and progress in the Christian life.

Chapter 4

The Right Way, the Wrong Way, and the Gospel Way

"By grace you live as the ones who have been saved, through faith; this is not something you do on your own, it is the gift of God, not the product of works in which one could boast" (Eph. 2:8-9).

There is an old saying in the Army, "There are three ways to do a thing: The right way, the wrong way, and the Army way." We said it in a rather derisive way. It seemed to us that when you got into the military, a perverse system of logic went into operation; the way people were placed in jobs and the way things functioned seemed contrary to common sense. But suppose we turn that thought to a positive purpose and suggest that there are three ways to live the Christian life: The right way, the wrong way, and the *gospel* way.

We know what the right way is. You follow the rules, you discipline yourself, you lead a good life. And we know the wrong way—slipshod, lukewarm, halfhearted, indifferent. But there is this third way too—the gospel way. The right way and the wrong way have this in common: They depend upon what *man* can or ought to do. The gospel way depends upon what *God* can do. A work done the gospel way is a work which is initiated and energized by God. The right way and the wrong way depend on men; the gospel way depends on God.

If we had to choose between living the right way and the wrong way, we would of course choose the right way, at least in our better moments! There are distinct advantages to the individual and society when we are disciplined, orderly, law abiding, and respectable in the way we conduct our life, the way we relate to one another in family, church, and community. But the right way and the wrong way are not our only alternatives. In fact, if we choose only between the right way and the wrong way, we head into one of the most serious problems the church faces, a problem which reoccurs in every religious awakening—the problem of *legalism*. We become bound under the law. God's answer to legalism is this glorious new way which He has created—the gospel way.

The Lord shared this with me in a personal and definite way when I was in my last year at seminary. It came unpremeditated while I was sitting in a class in Christian Ethics. My mind wandered somewhat from the lecture; I was thinking about what it would be like when I got out into a parish and became responsible for a flock. Then came the word: *"Expect nothing from people and everything from God."* Do not rest your hopes and expectations on the people in your congregation, nor on yourself and your own resources. But expect *everything* from God. That is the gospel way.

The Right Way

People who have been spiritually awakened seem to have an insatiable appetite for spiritual food. They go from meeting to meeting. Tonight a Bible study, tomorrow a prayer meeting, next Tuesday a guest speaker—they ferret them out. There are not enough days in the week to get in all the teaching they seem to crave. They soak it up like a sponge. They want to get as much of God's Word and God's teaching as they possibly can. They see that God sets down certain patterns, certain challenges for the kind of life that they ought to be living. They respond. They want to do the "right" thing.

What is the right way to behave in our personal life? Well, we should be loving, obedient, responsible, disciplined, concerned, involved—that kind of thing. But then it also comes down to specific requirements, expectations, or advice.

For instance, we are told that one of the basic things a Christian has to do is develop a discipline of prayer and Bible study. You can't live the Christian life apart from an expanding knowledge of God's Word. I once shared this idea with a woman in our congregation. It was a new idea to her. I suggested some simple procedures for daily devotions: Study a passage of scripture, write down the thoughts that come from this, and pray. For a period of several months, every Sunday morning she would hand me her week's notebook so I could see how she was doing. She wanted to do this the right way and she went at it with zeal and determination.

Or perhaps it comes to focus on a personal habit. Somebody hears a talk or a testimony that touches on the habit of smoking and decides, "I've got to quit smoking." The battle may be up and down but he keeps at it because he wants to do the right thing. One man virtually bit his tongue for six months trying to control his temper. (He got an ulcer doing it.) He wanted to do the right thing, even if it killed him. This is our natural human response. When God's Word addresses us we feel an obligation to do the right thing.

A woman once gave a talk about being honest and confessing anything that might be separating individuals in her audience. One of the listeners didn't get the whole message, but she wanted to do the right thing. She went up to the speaker afterward and said, "I just have to confess that I've always hated you." That is the kind of blunder that can happen when the "right way" dominates our thinking. The motive was good. She wanted to do the right thing. But the wisdom and direction of the Spirit was lacking.

The right way carries with it a certain compulsion to perform or achieve in relation to an accepted standard. The focus of one's interest is not so much on what or in relation to whom something is done, but on one's own record in doing it. It works at cross purposes with building personal relationships, including one's relationship with the Lord. It snares one in legalism, which one Catholic theologian accurately defined in this way: "Legalism is not the same as dedication and obedience. Legalism is looking to the Law [the "accepted standard"] rather than looking to the Lord."

The Wrong Way

There's also a wrong way to live. Most Christians could catalog that quickly. The lukewarm Christians Jesus speaks to in Revelation 3:14-22, the kind He wants to spit out of His mouth, were doing things the wrong way. They were just drifting along, probably Christians coming to church on Sunday, sharing somewhat in the life of the fellowship. But they kept Jesus in a nice, comfortable fenced-off position. They didn't want to deny Him outright, but neither did they give themselves to Him wholeheartedly.

More heartbreaking than the lukewarm Christian who has always been that way is the one who has moved into the things of God, then slidden back. Skeletons lie on the beach in the backwash of every renewal. They have reached in and tasted the goodness of God, then backed off. Maybe they had been trying hard to do the right thing, but somehow it got to be too heavy a load to carry and they slid back. And now they're going the wrong way.

These are the kinds of people Jesus talked about when He told the parable of the seed planted in shallow soil. It comes up quickly but when the sun beats down on it, when persecution comes, it wilts. Or the cares of the world begin to crowd in and their life is choked out. It's the wrong way. . . .

The Gospel Way

But what about this other way, the gospel way? If more people would move beyond the right way into the gospel way, they wouldn't get sidetracked on the wrong way. God never intended us to live the Christian life out of our own resources, out of our own good will and good intentions. God has made provision for us to live this life the gospel way.

What is the gospel way? One of the clearest presentations of it is found in Ephesians 2:8-10, "For by grace you have been saved through faith; and this is not your own doing, it is the gift of God—not because of works, lest any man should boast."

"By grace you have been saved." Though not an inaccurate translation, it is not fully descriptive of what the Greek says. The original text of that scripture says: "By grace you *are* the ones who have been saved." What the apostle is talking about here is not simply the grace that saved us; he's talking about the grace that *keeps* us. To paraphrase, "You are not living this life now by your own good intentions, you are not living the 'right way,' gritting your teeth and saying, 'I'll do it, I'll roll up my sleeves and do it.' No, but by *grace* you are living this life. By grace you are that one who has been saved and is now living that saved life. It's not because of works that you're able to do this. It's not because of your own effort and intention, your desire to obey God's law. It's by grace, it's by the outflowing of His mercy."

He goes on in verse 10 and tells us how this works out. "For we are *his* workmanship, created in Christ Jesus for good works." We are made for good works. A car is made to run, a drill is made to drill holes. We are made for good works, "which God prepared beforehand, that we should walk in them."

God has prepared the works that He wants us to do. Do you understand that? That good thing which He desires us to do has already been prepared that we might walk in it.

And as we walk in it God works in us—for by grace you *are* those who have been saved, by grace you *are walking* this life of discipleship. That's the gospel way.

What does this require of us practically? To begin with, simply a sensitivity to recongize the work which God sets before us. We must learn to recognize God's initiative. Then, as we walk in the work which He has prepared, He works in us—works *into* us—the character of Jesus. When the work is all done it's to the glory and credit of God. By His grace something of Jesus has been formed within us. Something of Jesus' character has been shaped and molded within us through that experience. The good work is not something we "do for God." It is an occasion for the Spirit to work something of Jesus into us.

If God has prepared for me a certain work and I jump over and start to walk in another work which He has not prepared, I am substituting the right way (or possibly the wrong way) for the gospel way. The gospel way has to do with the thing which God has initiated, the right way has to do with things that I myself determine to do. They are both "right" in the sense of being good and according to the general principles of Scripture; but one is self-chosen, the other is God-chosen.

When I go into a work which I myself choose to do, without waiting on the Lord, without sensing His leading and guidance, then I will be left to my own resources. God will just stand there with His arms folded and say, "Go ahead; you won't go to jail for it. It won't get you into any trouble in society or in the church. They may even pin a medal on you. Work yourself to a frazzle. And when you are all tired out and wondering why things have gone wrong, then come back to me and let me show you the work that I have prepared for you. . . ." In order to go the gospel way we must be sensitive to the *initiative* of the Lord.

The next step is to *believe*. We must expect that while we walk in sensitive obedience, God is working. My walking is only an invitation to God, an expression of faith. Everything depends on what the Lord does. "Lord, if you don't do the work inside of me while I'm walking in this, I will come out just as limited in my scope and vision as when I started out. But, Lord, if you work in me while I'm walking in this which you have prepared for me, then something is going to happen. Jesus is going to be formed in me." That's the gospel way.

When I was in the seventh grade the Lord touched my heart. I knew that part of being a Christian was to learn something about the Bible, so I went at it in a systematic and sensible way. I started at the beginning since that's where one starts most books. Each night I read a chapter in Genesis. It wasn't too long before I ran into the *begats* and that's where I got lost. I didn't even know what "begat" meant. I thought I was doing something spiritual, the right thing. But it wasn't the gospel thing. I hadn't yet learned how to sense a leading of the Lord.

By contrast, one year God led me into a quiet personal study of *Hebrews*. I went through that book verse by verse, in the original text. It sustained me in a difficult time. It required quiet discipline, but it was not difficult. I had the sense of being borne along by the Lord, of being involved in something which He had initiated. It was an exciting discovery each morning to sit down and study because I knew that He was at work. That's the gospel way. He initiates it, we walk in it, and as we walk in it He works in us.

The gospel way isn't difficult—it's *impossible*! It's impossible to live the gospel life out of our own resources. It's only as we walk in those good works which God has prepared beforehand, depending upon the functioning of His Spirit in us, that we can live this gospel life. But when God sets a work before us, and tells us to walk in it, He is ready to do the impossible in and through us.

Think of a man whose wife is uninterested in religious things. The man has been awakened. He finds a good church. He wants his wife to come but she has no time for it. He begins to learn something about God's order for his family. "I'm the head of the house. There are certain things I must do. I must give leadership, I must command."

So he says to his wife, not in a threatening way nor harshly, yet firmly, "I want you to come to church with me. I expect you to come."

He gets up on Sunday morning. "It's time to get ready for church," he tells his wife.

"Not for me," she replies, and rolls over in bed.

He gets dressed and goes by himself. And this continues—not just one or two Sundays but two years. He bears the humiliation of a wife who is rebellious against his authority. He has made it clear what he expects, but he doesn't try to force her because he knows that option is not open to him.

He walks in the humiliation of Christ who himself often has to put up with a rebellious bride, the church. He walks in the work which God has prepared for him. As he walks in that humiliation he trusts God, *and that trust is what gives God access to the wife.* The Spirit begins to work on her conscience, probe into her soul, and bring her to repentance, until the day he walks into that house and to his amazement she drops on her knees before him and says, "Forgive me for being a rebellious wife!"

That's the gospel way—not trusting our own strength or authority but trusting Jesus to do what we cannot do.

Lord, what is the gospel way for my life, for my family, for our church? What good work have you set before me this day? Lord, I want to walk in that work, because I know that when I do, something of eternal value will have been built into my life; something of Jesus will have been formed in me.

For by grace I am living this life, the life of one who has been saved. Not because of works. Then I would have something to boast about. For I am your workmanship, created in Christ Jesus for good works which you prepared beforehand that I might walk in them.

Chapter 5

Bite by Bite

One of the common notions which people have about Christians is that they are, or ought to be, holy, loving, and good. The truth of the matter is Christians are, or ought to be, *becoming* holy, loving, and good. And that makes a great difference.

Dr. Fredrik Schiotz, a former president of the American Lutheran Church, tells about the man who says, "I'm hungry enough to eat an elephant."

"Don't be silly," his friend says; "how could you eat an elephant?"

"Bite by bite," he replies.

And this is how God makes us holy: Bite by bite He offers us those elements of truth, those opportunities for obedience which make room in us for the holiness of Christ. You may be a long way from being a virtuoso in your spiritual life but that does not disturb God. The question He asks is simply this: have you made a start? Are you working at it? Have you taken the bite which is right in front of you? Are you going along with Christ each day, or have you settled down by the side of the road, letting God's plan for your life grind to a standstill?

Holiness: A Process

A little boy taking his first lessons on the violin is not a concert violinist. He isn't even ready for the Junior High School orchestra. He has simply taken the first steps toward *becoming* a concert violinist. An important step. An absolutely necessary step. But still a long way from his goal.

People outside the church register shock and dismay when a Christian behaves poorly. "Well! If that's the way a *Christian* acts, I want no part of it!" Christians themselves sometimes become terribly frustrated because their Christian life falls short of the standard set forth in the Bible.

The reason for this dismay or frustration stems from a wrong understanding of the Christian life. People think of it as something which just "is," something which has arrived. The truth of the matter is a Christian is simply on the way. The earliest designation of the Christian was that he was simply "a follower of the Way."

If the little boy who has had seven lessons on his violin plays a two-line song for Grandpa and Grandma who are visiting, they don't shake their heads and say, "I never heard such scratching and squeaking! And you say you are a violinist? I certainly don't think a violin ought to sound *that* way!" A violin has every right to sound that way when it's being played by a little boy with only seven lessons behind him. He *is* a violinist. Not a good one. Not one that a lot of people would want to listen to yet—just parents, a teacher, and members of the family, perhaps. But he keeps on. He listens to records of Nathan Milstein. He knows that he has a long way to go. Sometimes he gets frustrated because his progress seems slow. Sometimes he actually seems to be going backward rather than forward. Sometimes his teacher gets exasperated with him because he keeps making the same mistake over and over again. But the important thing is, he has started, he's on the way.

A Christian is not someone who has arrived but someone who has started in, someone who is on the way with Christ *and who stays at it.* He has believed in Jesus as the giver of salvation and has been born again into this new realm of the Spirit through faith in Christ. And now his life, his new life in Christ, begins in earnest.

"God's plan," St. Paul tells us, "is to make you holy."

That plan may begin with a crisis commitment, but the working out of that plan is a process, a lifelong process of going on with Jesus.

Don't look into a Christian congregation and expect to find anything like perfection. What you find is a lot of people who are *working* at the business of being a Christian, who are continuing to learn more and more of the life that pleases God. *The greatest indictment of a Christian congregation is not that it is falling short of the mark but that it has quit striving to reach the mark.*

Once God has brought you back into fellowship with himself, through the blood of Christ, He wants that fellowship to grow and develop. What purpose is there in creating life if that life never grows and develops?

A little baby that doesn't begin to grow and develop right away becomes a great anxiety to its parents. There is a parallel in the spiritual life: The first days and weeks of life are critical; if there is not immediate growth, the very life itself is in danger.

Some people point out the dangers involved in mass evangelism rallies. A lot of people get worked up to make a decision for Christ, and then two weeks later the campaign moves on and the people lapse right back into their old pattern of living. The danger is not that people get worked up and make a decision for Christ. A lot more people need to get worked up to that point! Every man born on earth needs to be brought to that choice. The danger comes if these people come away thinking there's nothing more. "Just go forward and make a decision for Christ. That's all there is to it." Actually, that is only the beginning. The danger comes when this new life which the Word of God has created doesn't begin to stretch out and grow. For this is the purpose God has in calling men to repentance and faith.

The First Step

The apostle Paul, writing to the church in Thessalonica,

outlines some important things about Christian growth.

"God's plan," he says, "is to make you holy, and that entails first of all a clean cut with sexual immorality" (1 Thess. 4:3, Phillips)

Thessalonica was a seaport town. Sexual immorality was common there, so that is what Paul deals with. But there is a spiritual principle involved which speaks to all of us, whether or not the particular issue in our life is the same as it was for the Thessalonicans.

First of all, Paul speaks to them as *fellow Christians*. He begins by saying, "We exhort you *in the Lord Jesus* . . ." (1 Thess. 4:1). In other words, "We come to stand beside you in the fellowship of the Lord who has redeemed us both." He does not stand up as a judge and consign them to hell for immorality. But neither does he do as so many do in our day, simply winking at the evil and thinking that thereby they are being "understanding" and "charitable." Paul's understanding is made of sterner stuff: "You must remember that God will punish all who offend in this matter, and we have warned you how we have seen this work out in our experience of life" (v. 6).

What Paul understands is that immorality is set against God's plan, which is to make us holy. Therefore he concludes that "anyone who makes light of the matter is not making light of a man's ruling but of God's command" (v. 8).

If Paul were coming to them merely as a friend, instead of as a Christian brother, he might just overlook the whole matter. Or, if he had a moralistic turn of mind, he might condemn them roundly. But coming as a Christian, Paul does neither. He speaks to them not as condemned sinners but as Christian brothers. Yet he tells them in straight, unvarnished terms that they must make a clean break with these immoral habits—and this he tells them precisely because they *are* his Christian brothers. He sees them as little children in the Christian life who do not yet fully realize that some habits and practices stunt Christian development. The habits must be cut off. Paul's concern is positive: that Christian growth not be hampered.

When we went out for football in high school, the coach laid down strict training rules: no smoking, no drinking, no late hours, no unexcused absences from practice. These were basic ground rules. No team can hope to become fully effective unless the team members make a clean break with these habits.

The same kind of thing holds true in the Christian life. You can't even begin with the ABC's of Christian living unless you are willing to break with the gross sins of the flesh—sexual immorality, gluttony, drunkenness, violent temper, dishonesty, and so on.

"Learn to control your body," Paul says. There are plenty of temptations in our culture today away from control of our bodies. But if we are serious about the business of going along with Christ, this is a basic decision which we have to make and keep. God's plan for making us holy can't get to first base until we face the issue of basic morality. That is the first step.

More and More

The first step is really kind of a negative one. The step that gets you going is this one: "Continue to learn more and more of the life that pleases God." And further on, in verse 10, "As regards brotherly love . . . we urge you to have more and more of this love!" There you have a picture of the Christian life in just three words: *more and more.* The purpose of the Christian life is that more and more of God's plan gets fulfilled in your life.

What is the purpose of my life? Why was I born? Why am I living? *To spend my years letting God make me holy,* cooperating with the Holy Spirit in His plan to develop this new life I have been given in Christ.

There is nothing quite so disheartening as a Christian who looks back over his life only to realize that he knows his

Lord no better now than the day he first accepted Him as Savior. Such a person is like the girl who played the lead in the class play, or the boy who starred on the basketball court . . . and then found all of life afterwards an anticlimax. God means us to grow. To paraphrase a part of 1 Corinthians 13, "When I was a child, a spiritual child, I spoke, thought, and reasoned like a child; but when I became a man in Christ Jesus, I put away childish things."

Every Christian congregation should have a few infants, a few babes in Christ—new, enthusiastic, exuberant Christians. But every congregation should also have in its midst the faith that is mature, ripened, tested, and proved through many experiences and trials. In the past few years a lot of new people have come to faith in Christ. But where is the ripened wheat? Where is the matured fruit? Where are those who have deep understanding of the Word of God because they have lived *in* it and lived *with* it and lived *by* it night and day? The church today stands in great need of "fathers in the faith," of "mothers in Israel" in whose lives mature fruit is evident.

God wants to make us holy. He wants to prune and refine and develop and mature us so that we can continue to come into new experiences with Him.

Our relationship with our children constantly changes as they grow older. We may have a relationship with our college-age son or daughter which was utterly impossible six years earlier. God wants our relationship with Him to grow in this same way. He'll go along with us in our early years as a Christian, talk baby-talk with us and pick us up when we fall down, but He doesn't want to baby-talk us through the whole of our Christian life. He wants us to go on to maturity.

One reason so many Christians get stunted in their spiritual life is because they miss the point that St. Paul gives us: "You must *continue to learn*." We want it to happen once for all and then all our troubles are over and we live happily ever after with Jesus. We may still have some struggles and developing to do as regards our worldly life, but our spiritual life just bumps along on a Sunday-to-Sunday basis.

This is not God's way. He makes you holy not in an instant but by a slow, patient, and *exhausting* process. And yet, Jesus does say, "My burden is *light*." He means that He doesn't burden you down with years of progress and expect you to handle it in a week of prayer and Bible study. He wants us to be content with the little tasks He puts before us. He wants us to take His plan for making us holy one step at a time. He finds joy in each small step we make toward maturity.

"God's plan is to make you holy." Bite by bite.

IV.

The Playing Board

To look at the Christian life as a duty is like wearing
blinders. We don't see how big the playing board really
is. On Square 1 God begins to remove the blinders. He
shows us the tremendous possibilities that are open to us if
we are willing to enter into them only and always
by the release of the Spirit.

Chapter 6

Get in the Flow
of Resurrection Power

In 1953, the football team at St. Olaf College in North-
field, Minnesota, powered its way to an undefeated season.
The star halfback on the team weighed less than 160
pounds. But he had learned a secret that more than made
up for his small stature—and proved devastating to the opposition.

Someone asked the coach what made his star halfback
so good. This is what he answered:

"He has speed, of course. But that's not the whole of
it—there are others as fast as he is. His real secret is the
way he follows his interference. He has an uncanny knack
for sensing just when the hole will open up, just where the
key block will be thrown. *He knows where the flow of power
is going, and he goes with it.*"

On the gridiron of life every advance we make is bitterly
contested. Not by people or circumstances, primarily. This
is a secondary factor. Our advance is contested, St. Paul
tells us, by principalities and powers, by spiritual hosts of
wickedness in heavenly places.

The contest on the gridiron of life is no light inter-squad
scrimmage. It's a hard-hitting battle with the powers of
Satan. To make yardage on *that* field you need power-plus.
But it doesn't stop with just having the power. Like the little St. Olaf halfback, you have to know how to *flow* with the
power.

When we talk about power on a gridiron we can mean a variety of things: speed, strength, agility, teamwork, precision timing. These are aspects of what we might call "football power." On the gridiron of life another kind of power is needed, a very special kind of power. St. Paul describes it in Ephesians 1:19-20: "I pray that you will begin to understand how incredibly great his power is to help those who believe him. *It is the same mighty power that raised Christ from the dead* and seated him in the place of honor at God's right hand in heaven" (TLB). The power we need when we step up to that scrimmage line against Satan is *resurrection power*. We need to know how to get into the *flow* of that power.

The Purpose, the Goal, of Resurrection Power

Every sandlotter knows the purpose of football power: You use it to score points against the other team. Everything the team does is directed toward the goal of winning a victory over the opposition. That goal provides the motive for every thought and every action on the gridiron.

Resurrection power has a purpose, too: to score points against man's arch-opponent, death. Death is Satan's triple-threat star. "Through fear of death we live all our lives as slaves to dread" (Heb. 2:15). Resurrection power moves resolutely toward the goal of a victory of life over death.

This becomes a check-point to help determine whether we are moving in the flow of resurrection power: Will it score points against death? Does it contribute to the victory of life over death?

Right at the center of the Christian faith lies the promise of eternal life. If what we are doing as Christians does not somehow undergird this basic purpose, then we will not be in the flow of resurrection power. But it involves more than a person saying sometime in his life, "I receive Jesus as my Savior." This is important, as important as getting suited up for a game, lining up for the kick-off, and getting started.

Jim Cavnar, one of the coordinators of the Word of God Community in Ann Arbor, Michigan, made an interesting statement in a workshop on evangelism. He said, "We have discovered that we need *five* spiritual laws. The first four lead a person to a knowledge of salvation. But it isn't enough for a person just to make a decision for Christ. The fifth spiritual law is that a person must come into a community of Christian people where that life is nourished. Until a person is an active member of a Christian fellowship, we don't consider him truly converted."

One can make a decision for Christ, but that doesn't mean he has won a victory over death. That life must be sustained and nourished. This is why it is important to ground our lives in those things that feed the resurrection life—prayer, study of His Word. This can go on privately, but it needs also to go on in a fellowship of believers.

Now a step further. You may be making plans to join a Bible study, and that is good. You will make advances against the enemy. You will penetrate his defenses. But if all your thoughts are focused on things like prayer and Bible study, you can still be thrown for a loss.

We once saw a high school team that ran from a double wingback formation and they did nothing but pass. The fullback got the snap from center and threw the ball on virtually every play. Naturally the team lost. They were too easily defensed.

There is a need for balanced offense. One of the balances we need in the Christian life is to engage not only in things like prayer and Bible study, but also in things that are a part of our total life experience. Christians need to learn how to play together, work together, socialize together. Satan is thrown off guard when God's people get together to share life in all its fullness and variety. God wants this kind of balanced offensive against the enemy.

The Position of Resurrection Power

Everyone from All-American to scrub knows on which

side of scrimmage to line up! The flow of power always begins on your own side of scrimmage. Before you can break through the enemy defenses, you have to line up with your own team, behind the line of scrimmage.

To get into the flow of resurrection power you must be properly positioned. You must be lined up with your teammates, your fellow believers. If you're out there doing your own thing, you may provide some entertainment for the spectators but you won't contribute to the victory. You'll never really get into the flow of resurrection power.

There is a need for God's people to be assembled together before they can move out against the enemy. Here we touch on a point that God is emphasizing in a way that He hasn't done for a long time, and that is in regard to the question of *authority.*

A football team got into the habit of talking in the huddle. Everybody had his own idea about which play should be called. When this got back to the coach at half time, he set it straight for them: "one voice in the huddle—the quarterback. If you see something at your position that will help him, let him know on the way back to the huddle. But when that huddle forms up, I want total silence except for the voice of the quarterback. It's his responsibility to call the play. I've worked with him on signal calling. I have confidence in him. It's the only way the whole team can move ahead."

This means that sometimes Christian people have to put up with a "second-best" plan. God allows that to happen. The perfect plan doesn't always take place in an assembly of God's people because those in positions of authority might not always see things as clearly as they ought to. That is one of the reasons leaders should always be open to counsel. Other "team members" may have important input which will help them arrive at a better decision. But any coach will tell you that it is better to use a second-best play and execute it well than to fumble through one that might have better potential.

This issue is so important with God that He allows people to come into a position where He says, "Accept this second-best plan, one that you don't personally agree with. It's more important for this team to get together than for your particular play to be used, even if it is a good one." With this approach we can move against the enemy with unity and strength.

There is nothing which so threatens the kingdom of Satan as a united team of believers. This throws fright into him and acts as a witness to the world. (See Phil. 1:27-28.) Tom Smails, a Scotch Presbyterian theologian, said, "The one thing the world can't do is live together, and that's the one thing the church should be showing them how to do."

The Potential of Resurrection Power

There are two levels of potential in a team: (1) The potential that resides in each individual player, with his unique talents, gifts, and abilities; (2) the potential that exists in the team, when all of these individual abilities are united and coordinated toward a common objective.

Resurrection power begins in the individual believer. "To *each* is given the manifestation of the Spirit" (1 Cor. 12:7). Resurrection power begins to flow when individual believers come to recognize the gifts and power in one another, and depend upon that power as they move out together against the enemy.

The little halfback at St. Olaf was so well acquainted with the tactics and style of the man who ran interference for him that he'd make his cut before the man actually threw his block, then flash past before the opponent could recover and tackle him. We need to become so well acquainted with each other that we know each other's gifts and abilities and learn to depend on them—and they on us. This is how we get into the flow of resurrection power. Resurrection power isn't something that flows simply through the individual. There is a flow of resurrection power available to a body of believers that an individual can never touch. There is a flow of resurrection power available in the whole body of Christ that no single congregation can touch. And this is what God is aiming for. He wants us to get the feel of being a part of His great team so that we can flow with a power that overpowers all the power of the enemy.

Chapter 7

Is Your Faith Out of Breath?

Have you ever said, "I wish I had faith like St. Paul"? Or have you seen someone like Billy Graham addressing a throng of people, so alive and vibrant and sure of his Christian experience that you feel a twinge of envy and wished that your faith could be like that?

Dynamic Christians have discovered the secret of a vital Christian faith which James recorded long ago, "Faith by itself, if it has no works, is dead" (James 2:17). The nature of this death is described as follows: "For as the body, apart from the spirit [or the breath] is dead, so faith apart from works is dead" (2:26). Faith is like the body, and works is like the breath of the body. If the breath leaves the body, the body dies. The good works that a Christian does are like a breath of life to him. Works give life to our faith.

When I was in the army I coached a football team. It was made up of a variety of men, from those who had played semi-professional football to those who had never even had a football in their hands. One fellow on the team had played some semi-professional ball. He was stocky and fast—a terrific guard. But he wasn't much good to the team. He was out of shape. After the third play he was all out of breath. He'd wave to the sidelines, "Take me out, Coach, I've played my game." So there he sat on the bench, useless, because he didn't have the breath.

That kind of thing can happen to faith. It can get sluggish, it can get out of form. It can get short of breath.

Christ in You

What is faith? The most common idea of faith is that I mentally agree with an idea, maybe going a little deeper, that I have a feeling of trust regarding something, such as trusting that the chair I am sitting in is going to hold me. But the faith that the Bible speaks about goes much deeper than that. *Through faith Christ is present and alive within me.* Faith is more than knowing about Jesus, more than believing in Jesus as Savior. It involves opening the door, so that the living Spirit comes into you and *lives within you.*

That is what the Bible means by faith. Paul says, "God chose to make known how great among the Gentiles are the riches of the glory of this mystery, which is Christ in you, the hope of glory" (Col. 1:27). That's the miracle of the Christian. The Christian has *within himself* the living God. When you have God within you, then, and only then, do you have real faith. "It is no longer I who live, but Christ who lives in me; and the life I now live in the flesh I live by faith in the Son of God, who loved me and gave himself for me" (Gal. 2:20).

This is what makes Christianity different from other religions. Christianity isn't a philosophy of life, although it has a philosophy. It isn't a set of moral values, although it has moral values. Other religions in the world set up certain standards, certain ways of thinking, requiring that you follow them in order to be a member in good standing.

But not so with our faith. We enter a relationship with Jesus, a living person, unseen, immortal, real. When we read about Christians who have done great things for the Lord, we don't see people who merely have thought things out clearly or who have lived exemplary lives, but we see people who have had a relationship with Christ. When John Wesley went to Aldersgate he heard the reading of Martin Luther's commentary on the letter to the Romans. As he listened his heart was "strangely warmed." The living presence of Christ began to burn and vibrate within him, and the faith that the Bible speaks about came to life.

Christ Working Through You

The Christ who is now in you becomes active and begins to do things in you and through you. That is what works are. A good work is more than doing something just because you know it's the thing to do. It is actually this living Christ within you beginning to make His presence felt, acting out His purposes, His desires, His will through you.

When a work is truly Christian—in other words, when it is Christ within us working out His life—then it is going to draw attention to Him. Jesus said, "Let your light so shine before men, that they may see your good works [And say what a nice person you are? No.] . . . and give glory to your Father who is in heaven" (Matt. 5:16).

Jesus did His great works in such a way that He turned the focus upon God, and the people gave glory to God. When the work is truly Christian, when Christ is working it out through us and in us, inevitably He is going to turn people's eyes to God.

Jesus never wanted people simply to look at Him. He wanted them to see God working in and through Him. When the New Testament speaks about good works in a positive sense, it means Jesus doing something through your body, using your body as an instrument. "Yield yourselves to God . . . and your members to God as instruments of righteousness" (Rom. 6:13). Become a tool in His hands.

The Breath of Life

We know that Christ is alive within us, and yet too often we find ourselves back under the old burden of the law— doing things just because it's our *duty* to do them. The joy of serving Christ and of letting His life flow through us seems like a dream. We can't get hold of it.

We need to develop a new attitude toward the works

that God puts in front of us. Instead of looking at these works as things that we are supposed to do because a Christian does these things, the Bible encourages us to look upon every work before us as an opportunity, as God's offer of vital faith.

If a person has been suddenly struck in the midsection and the breath has been knocked out of him, he is ready for some help. He wants his breath back. Similarly, one whose faith in Christ is at a low ebb needs works. The work that God sets in front of us is like a deep breath to the person who is out of breath.

When God made man He formed him out of the dust of the earth, He formed him in all his parts, and then He breathed into him the breath of life. Then man became a living soul. We may have faith in Christ, but it's dead until the good works of Christ have been breathed into it.

A tree is known by its fruits. It has a certain nature, and it produces fruit according to its nature. Since a Christian has Christ within him, it is his nature to produce the works of Christ. But if the faith is there and yet is not alive, something has to be breathed into it. "Faith was active along with Abraham's works, and faith was completed by works" (James 2:22).

God made Adam out of the dust. He made him for a definite purpose, and then He breathed upon him and Adam came alive. He created you and me in Christ Jesus for good works, and now He comes and takes these good works which He has prepared and sets them in front of us, like a breath of life. They give life to faith. You can have the same faith that Abraham had because, like him, you can trust God and walk in the works God sets before you.

Out of Breath?

Peter thought he had great faith. He promised, "Lord, I am ready to go with you to prison and to death." Jesus replied, "Peter, the cock will not crow this day, until you three times deny that you know me" (Luke 22:33-34).

But after the resurrection Jesus came to Peter and offered to restore his faith. How did He do it? How did He offer to revitalize that shaken faith of Peter's?

Peter probably went through tremendous turmoil of soul, wondering if he would ever again be useful to God. Jesus came to this Peter, whose faith was all out of breath, and breathed upon him. He gave him new breath. How? By putting before him a work. He said, "Feed my sheep." By setting before Peter that good work of feeding His sheep He gave him the opportunity to receive a revitalized faith (see John 21:15-19).

Is your faith out of breath, as Peter's was? God offers you a new breath of life. After you've fed on God's Word, He puts you into circumstances in home and neighborhood that offer you the chance to let Jesus live through you. God offers you a new breath of life. Take it. Breathe deeply of that good work. Walk into it as you would walk into a bracing wind. The secret of a vital Christian faith is to enter into the work that God sets before you. It is the breath of life to Christ who lives within you.

Chapter 8

The Notre Dame Football Talk

I guess I belong to that generation of football fans that constitute a kind of "spiritual alumni" of Notre Dame University. With me this began at an early age, because my father was a football coach. While other children were being raised on stories like Jack and the Beanstalk or Three Billy Goats Gruff, I was hearing about the glories of Knute Rockne and the Four Horsemen of Notre Dame.

But football was more than a game in our family; it was an endlessly varied parable of life. My father could enter into almost any discussion of philosophy or religion with some appropriate illustration from football.

We would kid him about this, but he had a game retort: "I'm in good company. The apostle Paul loved athletic metaphors. He said that he was one who 'did not box as one beating the air . . . he ran so as to win the prize, . . . and there was laid up for him the wreath of victory . . . !'"

Indeed, teaching about the Kingdom of God comes across to us most clearly through metaphor. In the thirteenth chapter of Matthew we see the Kingdom compared to mustard, leaven, a seed sown in a field. It is not inappropriate for us to think about the Kingdom in terms of a metaphor. In order to shed light on a particular aspect of the Kingdom, I'm going to suggest a metaphor from the realm of athletics:

The Kingdom is like a group of people who came together under a coach, who molded them into a team that moved with such precision and order and astonishing innovation that they overcame all of their opponents.

The game of football combines two contrasting elements which in the kingdoms of this world rarely strike the right kind of balance: The elements of *order* and *freedom*. When order becomes too repressive, the cry has always gone up for freedom. And when freedom has become irresponsible, the cry has gone up for order.

If you and I were to draw up a blueprint for the perfect kingdom, certainly these two elements would be foundational. We would want a kingdom in which there was freedom, yet also order and security.

That is what the Kingdom of our Lord Jesus Christ offers to us. Jesus said, "If the Son shall make you free, you shall be free indeed." Perfect freedom. Yet it says also that God "has put all things under his feet," in perfect order.

How does Jesus accomplish this? Let's consider it in the light of this metaphor. What happens when a football squad comes together under a coach?

Rules

First of all, there are rules. The rules of the game establish basic order.

What happens if players begin suddenly to run out of bounds, to slug and clip at will? The game breaks down, possibly bearing some resemblance to the old game, but in reality something different has evolved.

Life in the Kingdom operates according to certain basic ground rules. These fall into two categories. First of all there are general rules—rules that apply everywhere and at all times. These are the cardinal doctrines of the faith and the moral law.

What does a football team do in regard to the rules? How much time do they spend on the rules? Not very much. They quickly learn the rules and get into the business of preparing for the game. They don't sit around and endlessly debate the rules.

What would happen to a team that spent half its time wondering whether the rules were valid, whether they might not set up a better set of rules, whether the rules really apply any more? They would be defeated, because other teams that accept the rules for playing the game would put together a team that would beat them.

One of the issues that has given real strength to the charismatic renewal is the fact that it has accepted the basic ground rules without debate. I can't recall ever participating in a charismatic teaching session or prayer group where there was a basic argument about any of the cardinal doctrines of the Christian Faith, such as justification by faith, the virgin birth, the atonement, the divinity of Christ, the validity of the moral law. All of these things are accepted without question. Critics sometimes fault charismatics for not spending enough time on the "rules," or basics, apparently failing to recognize how thoroughly "the rules" are believed and accepted; therefore it isn't necessary to spend a lot of time on them.

This is a stance an individual believer or a renewal movement should be jealous to maintain. A word of prophecy came at a Notre Dame Catholic Charismatic Conference: "I will no longer hold back while my people are being deceived." There are deceiving words going out in our day saying that the rules don't apply any longer. Another prophecy said, "I will set aside the false prophet and the false teacher"—those who want to rewrite the rules and change the game.

A group of Presbyterian ministers made a covenant that if their church comes to the place where it legitimizes homosexuality as a valid alternative life-style, at that point, in conscience, they would have to separate from their church. Across the broad denominational spectrum of the charismatic renewal, there is a solid stance against the taking of innocent life, against abortion. The historic morality of the Christian faith is not debated; it is accepted as a basic ground rule with which one moves out into life.

There is a second category or aspect of the rules. There

are not only the general rules that apply to everybody; there are also things that we might call local customs. There is a little town in northern Minnesota that couldn't find a level piece of ground longer than 80 yards, so their football field was 80 yards long. When other teams came to play them they had to adapt their strategy and style to an 80-yard field.

There are varieties within the body of Christ—forms of worship, life-style and piety. These are things we have to recognize in one another and regard with respect.

Sometimes we get a little uneasy because other people's customs are different from ours. The story is told of a group of female parish workers who had a meeting during the Lutheran World Federation Convention in Hanover, Germany, in 1952. They had come from all over the world and wanted to get together to share their ideas and experiences. When the American parish workers came in wearing rouge and lipstick, the Danish parish workers were so scandalized that they almost dropped their cigars. . . .

One of the moods that's abroad in our age is that customs are foolish and everybody should do his own thing. That's not the way you play the game. Customs are not to be scorned. They are to be respected. St. Paul said, "When I'm with the Jews, I'm like a Jew. When I'm with the non-Jews, I'm like them. I'm all things to all men." I translate that into two simple words: *good manners.*

Charismatics need to heed that kind of an admonition. It's easy to go home from a conference where one has worshipped in a style maybe somewhat different than in the local parish, and want to go in and do one's charismatic thing. Good manners would dictate sensitivity. When, out of love, one is sensitive to the local customs that prevail, it does not quench the Spirit; it releases the Spirit in a wonderful way.

At the Lausanne World Congress on Evangelism in 1974, I was asked to chair a workshop on charismatic renewal. People from a variety of traditions attended this workshop, not all of them sympathetic to the charismatic movement.

A man from Scotland shared his experience of being renewed in the Holy Spirit in a different tradition than the Pentecostal or charismatic tradition. He had, in fact, been hostile to the Pentecostal tradition. He preached against speaking in tongues from the pulpit, saying it was of the devil. This went on for several years.

There was one young woman in his congregation, he said, "of such a sweet spirit that if anyone had the Holy Spirit in fullness it was that girl." One day when he was fulminating against speaking in tongues, one of his deacons said to him, "But don't you know that Sister Jean speaks in tongues?" The pastor commented, "You could have blown me over with a feather!" He went to this young woman and asked whether this report were true. She answered, "Yes, praise God, it is true." Again the man commented, "But she was so humble and so sweet-spirited that knowing there was no interpreter in the congregation, she maintained her silence." The man concluded by asking forgiveness of his Pentecostal brethren for the wrong he felt he had done them. That was the fruit, in part, of that young woman who was willing to behave according to the customs of that particular congregation, and simply exhibit good manners.

The rules do not deny our freedom; they simply define it, designate where and how that freedom is to be exercised.

Fundamentals

Knute Rockne, the legendary coach at Notre Dame, said that the game of football consists of blocking, tackling and running—the fundamentals; learn them and never forget them. That means that you submit to personal training and discipline. A good coach insists on fundamentals.

My father attended the first coaching school that Knute Rockne ever held. On the second day of that coaching school Rockne said, "This afternoon we are going to have some drills on fundamentals. I want every one of you out here in football togs. You can get them from the locker room."

Some of these men had been coaching longer than Rockne himself. They didn't take him seriously. "We didn't come here for that," they grumbled. "We came here to get some of his plays, his strategy, his style. . . . "

That afternoon only three men showed up in football uniforms. The rest of them learned something about Rockne's style.

He lined them up and began to walk down the line. He came to a silver-haired man in a dark business suit. "Nice suit you have there," said Rockne. "I like the tie, too; goes well with the suit." Then with a roar, "You'd make a good tackle—get out there!"

They found out Rockne wasn't a man you said "No" to. He lined them up and said, "When I blow my whistle the first time, start running down the field; when I blow it the second time, hit the dirt and roll!" He blew the whistle once and they started running; he blew it again and the line of nicely dressed coaches rolled in the dirt. Two hours later there was etched into the memory of those coaches a lesson they would never forget: *You never get beyond fundamentals.*

No matter how far you progress in the Christian life, you must continue to give attention to the basics. In the Christian life it means things like this: substantial time in daily prayer; serious and regular study of the Word; correction of what is sinful and untrue in our lives; solidifying our immediate personal relationships. These are fundamentals that we can never neglect, never move beyond.

We run into two dangers when we are dealing with fundamentals. The first danger is that we ourselves begin to neglect the fundamentals and get sloppy. Don't grow weary. Persevere in the normal, daily duties.

The second way in which we neglect the fundamentals is that we begin to take them for granted in others. Because we have gone through a lot of the fundamentals, we don't give the kind of attention we should to helping other people. We lose the sense of joy and discovery, and the adventure of participating with others as they enter into things that we may have entered into in previous years.

The fundamentals include discipline, a high order of discipline and obedience. Only discipline leads to real freedom, which is the freedom to do the thing God calls us to do.

One of the things we have to be delivered from is the idea that everything we do in life ought to be interesting and exciting. Some things are just routine, and that's normal and acceptable. Many mornings during my prayer time I tell the Lord, "Lord, I sure am bored today. I don't feel like much of anything. But, Lord, I'm going by your Word. I'm going by what you have told me, not the way I feel."

God is preparing us for things that only people who have mastered the fundamentals will be able to enter into, and that's where the real excitement is.

Team Work

The third thing a football team needs is team work. Team work means that you are ready to sacrifice personal preferences for that which will benefit the whole body.

This calls, first of all, for a radical appreciation of one another. This is more than saying, "They are nice people. I have no prejudices against them. I think they have a fine life, a fine ministry." No, it is *radical* appreciation, which means that you recognize that your life depends on their life, that your life is incomplete apart from your being united and interdependent with them. Radical appreciation of one another means that you recognize that you cannot exist apart from one another.

When Knute Rockne developed his famous Notre Dame shift, it absolutely pulverized the opposition. Grandland Rice dubbed the Notre Dame backs, "The Four Horsemen." They ran roughshod over the opposition. The sports writers went wild in their praise and adulation.

But Rockne, master psychologist that he was, noticed something happening on the team. In one of the games he pulled out the first string line, which another sports writer had humorously dubbed, "The Seven Mules." Now the Four Horsemen were running behind the second string line, and things didn't go too well. Notre Dame got pushed around the first half.

Rockne came into the locker room at half time and found the Four Horsemen sitting rather dejectedly over in a corner. He went up to them and said, "What's the matter, boys? Didn't you show them your press clippings?" That afternoon the Four Horsemen learned to appreciate the Seven Mules in a radical way!

When Cardinal Suenens of Belgium invited a group of ecumenical observers to have tea with him after the final Eucharist at the Catholic Charismatic Conference in Rome in May 1975, Dr. Rodman Williams, a Presbyterian theologian, said to him, "What has happened in Rome is not only of significance to the Roman Catholic Charismatic Renewal; it's of significance to the whole renewal; it's as significant to us as Presbyterians as it is to you as Catholics."

That's a distinctive feature of this renewal: A recognition that God is bringing together treasures from His whole body; the wounded body of Christ is being truly knit together in the Spirit and by the Spirit.

Team work involves eager obedience—obedience to the coach and his staff. Only the coach and his staff can mold the individual performers into a team. It's at this point that we grasp the secret both of order and of freedom.

The order and the freedom of God's kingdom is found in our relationship to the Lord and those whom the Lord has set over us. We see this illustrated beautifully in Mark 2:23-28. Jesus is walking through the grain fields on the Sabbath, and His disciples pluck a few heads of grain and begin to eat. The Pharisees come along and say, "Why are you allowing your disciples to do what is unlawful? That's against the law of the Sabbath."

This was the spirit of legalism, which is order gone overboard. Legalism says we can't relax the rules one iota. If we do, chaos will result. *Legalism looks to the law for its security.*

The opposite of that is libertinism, which is freedom gone berserk. Libertinism says, "Fie on your rules! I don't care about rules. I want to know what will make me happy right now." "Every man does what is right in his own eyes."

Jesus, in this encounter, steers a middle course between these two extremes. He does it in an interesting way. He says, "Don't you remember how David went to Abiathar, the high priest, when he and his men were hungry; and they ate of the bread of the Presence, which was not lawful for any but the priests to eat?"

Notice how carefully Jesus chooses His setting. He doesn't tell a parable about "Isaac, the local sheepherder." It's David, the anointed of the Lord and the high priest of the Lord. These two men together reckon that here is a situation that calls for flexibility; here indeed is a situation that calls for an exception to the rule.

What kept the disciples of Jesus, at this point, from careening off into libertinism? "Whoopee, the Sabbath rules are out! We can do what we want on the Sabbath." The thing that kept them from doing that was their relationship to the Lord, and His high regard for the law.

A legalist looks to the law for security. A libertine looks to his own immediate satisfaction. *But a disciple looks to his Lord.*

Jesus did not give a new law to replace the law of the Pharisees. "Forget the law of the Pharisees. I'll tell you how to keep the Sabbath, and in 24 easy steps." *No, He gave himself as an administrator of the law.*

One of the responsibilities of God-appointed leaders is to administer the law with wisdom. That means to enforce the law and bring thereby the benefits of order and security to God's people. It also means to adapt the law to special situations, where the law simply doesn't fit.

God's answer to libertinism is a leader who respects the law. My father once told the story of a coach who watched his halfback break loose and head for paydirt down the sideline. As he went across the double stripe the official threw up both hands, signaling a touchdown. But when the runner had gone by his own team's bench, his outside cleat had ticked the chalkline—he had gone out of bounds. In the excitement nobody had seen it, except the player's own coach. The coach walked out onto the field and said to the official, "My boy went out of bounds when he came by our bench." So the touchdown was called back. That was a leader who respected the law.

The law isn't something out there to "get us." Our own Coach insists upon the law because He knows that if we bend the law, break the law, abuse the law, we bring disgrace upon God and His people. And so the answer that God gives to libertinism is a leader who regards the law highly.

On the other hand, God's answer to legalism is a leader who loves his people. One day as my father was sitting in his office one of his former athletes came in. He held in his hand a trophy as a gift to my father. On the trophy was inscribed, "Carleton—St. Olaf, 1932." (St. Olaf was the college where my father coached, and Carleton was its archrival.)

"I remember that game," my father said. "We lost, 6-2."

"Yes, that's right," the man said. "And the reason we lost is because I fumbled on the two-yard line. I was a freshman, and you let me play in this one non-conference game where freshmen were eligible. You had worked with me on the way I carried the ball. I had a tendency to let it float out from my body and you told me how to carry it tucked in close. On that play I didn't remember the coaching. A hole opened up on the two-yard line wide enough for a truck to drive through, and I fumbled. We lost the ball, and we lost the game. But the thing I have never forgotten was that you didn't take me out of the game. You seemed to recognize in that situation that I needed another chance."

A leader has to know when a situation comes up which you can't simply take care of "out of the book." That is God's answer to legalism. Not a whole set of other rules to counter the rules that aren't fitting, but a leader who loves his people.

God is calling forth a people who are going to live out their lives in radical obedience, and to those He promises both order and freedom. Certainly men and women in leadership will make mistakes, will need to ask forgiveness, will need correction. But obedience is still God's appointed way to mold a group of individuals into a team.

Strategy

Strategy means moving in a coordinated and effective way to accomplish the Lord's purpose. We need to move from the question of what to do in a church service or at a prayer meeting to supporting each other's lives. We need to clarify our understanding of authority, of mission. Communities need to help and support one another.

God is sounding a death knell to an irresponsible individualism. Again a word of prophecy: "The foundation of my Kingdom is my people who are willing to lay down their lives for one another." This is strategy, the Lord's strategy.

Successful strategy depends on two things. It depends, first of all, on people who can follow orders.

The story is told of Bear Bryant, the great coach at Alabama. He once had a quarterback who was the slowest runner on the squad but was an exceptional passer. He never ran with the ball. He only handed it off to the other backs and passed.

In one game Alabama was ahead by just six points, and the clock had less than two minutes to run. He sent this quarterback in with the instruction to play it safe and run out the clock. The quarterback came into the huddle and said, "The coach says we should play it safe, but that's what the other team is expecting. Let's give them a surprise." So he called a pass play. He dropped back and threw, and the defending halfback, a sprint champion, knifed in, intercepted, and headed for a touchdown.

The quarterback took after him, ran him down from behind at the five-yard line, and saved the game. After the game the opposing coach came up to Bear Bryant and said, "What's this business about your quarterback not being a runner? He ran down my speedster from behind."

"Well," said Bryant, "your man was running for six points. My man was running for his life."

The Lord is calling forth a people who can follow through with what they're told to do. A word of prophecy: "We have been standing before the King receiving orders. We must begin to put these orders into effect." Successful strategy depends upon people who can follow orders.

Successful strategy also depends upon people who can exercise initiative. One of the famous stories about Knute Rockne tells about him sending in a substitute quarterback with the instruction, "I want you to run two plays and then punt." The quarterback ran an off-tackle slant, the man broke into the open and gained 30 yards. The next play went around the other end and brought them down to the two-yard line. And then, to the horror of the Notre Dame fans, the man dropped back and punted. He followed orders, but the situation called for initiative.

Along with a call to obedience, the Spirit also calls His people to courageous innovation. "I call you to something new and you must lay down your resistance. It will be costly. It will be painful. But I will be with you."

Now we have set forth the truth that we must follow orders, and illustrated it with the case of a man who decided to exercise initiative and got in trouble. We set forth the truth that we must exercise initiative, and illustrated it with the case of a man who followed orders and got into trouble. We have done that for a reason. The last thing in the world we want to convey is the idea, "Ah, I have learned a new principle by which I will always know when to follow orders and when to exercise initiative." There is no such principle.

If we could do it ourselves, all we would need is a book of rules—just give me the book and I can play the game. What each of those quarterbacks needed was a closer association with his coach, a better understanding of his mind and his mentality so he could handle the situation that he faced.

Only Jesus himself, by His Holy Spirit, can give us the steadfastness to follow orders and the courage to exercise initiative in the right kind of a way. Learning the rules will not bring in the Kingdom. Mastering the fundamentals will not give us the Kingdom. Teamwork will not secure for us the Kingdom. Successfully executing a strategy will not guarantee the Kingdom. Only one thing, Jesus Christ himself, will bring in the Kingdom.

Thy Kingdom Come: "The Kingdom of God comes indeed without our prayer, but we pray in this petition that it may come also among us." Even so, Lord Jesus, also among us!

V.

The Stack of Cards

It's the mixture of life and death that is hard. By nature we would choose to be completely one or the other—either miracle worker or martyr, but not both at the same time. To be set down on Square 1 when we're all fired up, and then to be released when we feel weak and helpless—that is the frustration and the glory of the Spirit-led life.

Chapter 9

I Will Restore

There is a period in British history referred to as "The Restoration." It followed a time when the royal family had been put off the throne. In "The Restoration" the king was restored to the throne.

Restoration involves conflict. The Rightful King has been denied His kingship. A pretender has taken over. Restoration challenges the pretender's claim. It puts him off the throne and restores the Rightful King to His place of rule.

When God decrees restoration we find ourselves suddenly back on Square 1. God will tolerate neither our rebellion nor our self-assured virtue when either seeks to lay claim to the throne of Christ. When God says, "I will restore," He lays down a challenge to every pretender to the throne of Christ. "I will put down every pretender and enthrone my Anointed One as King of kings and Lord of lords!"

The Arch-Pretender—and His Cohorts

Who is the Pretender? The Arch-Pretender is the devil, sure enough. But he is always seeking to enlist allies, tempting us as he tempted our first parents, "You shall be like God! You shall be the one in charge!" When we yield to that temptation we become men of the flesh rather than men of the Spirit, pretenders along with the devil.

Restoration certainly does involve God's conquest over

Satan. But there is an aspect of restoring the king to his throne that is as close to us as the hand at the end of our wrist. Because one of the most persistent pretenders to the throne of Christ is what the Bible calls "the flesh." When the Bible speaks of "the flesh" in this way, it means our entire human nature lured into rebellion against God. Whenever God's people experience restoration, the flesh must be dealt with, and dealt with decisively.

Perhaps we have not thought of ourselves as anything so awesome as pretenders to the throne of Christ. But perhaps also we have not experienced the full measure of restoration that God has for us. Perhaps we have missed the full power and blessing of Christ's rule among us because sometimes we are pretenders without even realizing it.

Our personal participation in God's work of restoration will be in direct proportion to how decisively our own flesh is dealt with. When God deals with the flesh, it opens the way to a fuller experience of the reality and power of God. When the power of the pretender is dealt with, the power of the Rightful King is released.

There are two little sentences of eight words that epitomize the struggle between the Pretender and the Rightful King. The eight words that signal the Pretender's assault upon the throne of Christ may never have occurred to you in quite the following way, yet in essence they constitute the assault of the flesh upon the throne of Christ: "Let me tell you what *I* can do." That's the phrase that needs to be thrown down.

When we give up that phrase there is another one that needs to replace it, expressing the surrender of our human nature to the lordship of Christ: "Tell me what *You* are going to do."

In these two simple phrases is pictured the struggle between the Pretender and the Rightful King. Does it sound too simple? Consider how practically and decisively it deals with our Christian life in three basic areas: the area of our *justification*, the area of our *sanctification*, and the area of our *ministry*.

Justification

Justification has to do with our citizenship in God's Kingdom. How do we qualify?

The royal edict on kingdom citizenship is this: It shall be a *free gift*. It includes a number of things. It includes sonship, forgiveness, righteousness, eternal life. And it is given freely—not a word in the Bible about earning or deserving it.

Right here that Pretender, the flesh, turns up and mounts his little eight-word assault, *"Let me tell you what I can do*. It's nice to receive grace, but I can add something to that. I can contribute something of my own to this business of salvation."

This is a pretender that God dealt with through the Reformers. They stood against this particular attempt of the Pretender to push Christ off the throne. They said, "We are not going to take part in this rebellion." In their documents they take an uncompromising stand against any pretender who would seek to add anything to Christ's work of redemption: "It is taught among us that we cannot obtain forgiveness of sin and righteousness before God by our own merits, works, or satisfactions, but that we receive forgiveness of sin and become righteous before God by grace, for Christ's sake, through faith, when we believe that Christ suffered for us and that for his sake our sin is forgiven and righteousness and eternal life are given to us" (The Augsburg Confession).

This Pretender has been around for a long time, and is still with us today. A few years ago a research project among Lutherans discovered that more than half of the Lutherans in the United States believe that their standing with God rests partially upon their own good works. This in a church that takes its name from the man who raised the standard of justification *by faith*!

When the issue is our justification, we have to quit telling God what we think we can do and listen when He tells us what He is ready to do. And what He is ready to do is justify us freely, for Christ's sake.

This has to become practical. One way that it has become practical in my own experience is in my daily prayers. I like to begin my prayers on the ground of my justification. I like to start out each day on the basis of the blood of Jesus, sing some songs about the blood, declare before God that I'm here on one basis only, and that is the atonement of Christ. I'm here because I'm His child by grace. I don't care what kind of a day I had yesterday, what kind of a day I'm looking forward to today. It's the unassailable work of Christ that gives me access into the presence of the Father this new day—hallelujah!

We have to be alert to the subtle schemes of the Pretender to *rob Christ of His glory* by getting us to trust in anything else than in Him alone for our salvation, for our justification. It slips subtly into our thinking. "Lord, I know I muffed it yesterday, but let me tell you what I am planning to do today. . . . Lord, I know I made some mistakes, but look at all the good things I did. . . . George, if you want to get right with God you've got to start reading your Bible and go to church."

We need to feel the sharp point of the sword of the Spirit at our throat. This is warfare! Resist that little eight-word assault. Kneel down, surrender, and give voice to the words that token our surrender, "Tell me what *You* are going to do."

What He is going to do is give us free, unmerited grace. That is how the Rightful King handles our justification.

Sanctification

Sanctification has to do with how we live our life, how we behave as citizens of God's kingdom. This gets right down to the daily business of how we treat members of our family, how we manage our finances, how we drive on the freeway, how we pray, how we help those in need.

The royal edict on Kingdom living is, "Be perfect as your heavenly Father is perfect" (Matt. 5:48).

That life which is planted in us as a free gift has a way of expressing itself. It expresses itself in obedience. Paul said that he was given his apostleship "to bring about the obedience of faith" (Rom. 1:6).

How are we able to do this? In the gift of eternal life we receive the Holy Spirit as our enabler, giving us power to live the life that He calls us to live. "God has done what the law, weakened by the flesh, could not do: sending his own Son in the likeness of sinful flesh and for sin, he condemned sin in the flesh, in order that the just requirement of the law might be fulfilled in us, who walk not according to the flesh [not in the tracks of the Pretender], but according to the Spirit [subjects of the Rightful King]" (Rom. 8:3-4).

Here again the Pretender mounts his little eight-word assault, "Let me tell you what I can do. You can't expect me to be perfect, but I'll do my best." This is the Pretender that God has had to deal with down through the history of the church. The apostle Paul speaks to the people who are thinking about these very things. "Since we are saved by grace, shall we sin the more that grace may abound?" (Rom. 6:1). All through the history of the church we find people who hear this word about holy living and take a stand against that old Pretender, the flesh, that wants to water down Christ's call to obedience.

This old Pretender is a sly fox. He will actually make his bid for the throne disguised as an ally of the Rightful King. You will hear him say things like this, "If you stress obedience and righteousness too much it undercuts grace, and we want to live by grace." That is a phony claim. Because the God who offers free, unmerited grace is the same God who calls us to unconditional obedience. It's the Pretender who tries to water down grace in justification, and obedience in sanctification.

When the issue is our sanctification, we have to quit telling God what we can or cannot do in our own strength and let Him tell us what He can do; and that is to call us and empower us to live lives of righteousness and holy obedience.

We have to be alert for every attempt of this Pretender *to rob Christ of His glory* by getting us to water down our obedience to the level of our human will and intention. We need to feel the sharp point of the sword of the Spirit against our throat, surrender, humble ourselves before the Lord and say, "Lord, what are *You* going to do?"

What He is going to do is call and enable us to live, by the Spirit, lives of holy obedience.

Ministry

Ministry has to do with our service or calling in the Kingdom. How do we minister as servants and representatives of Christ?

The royal edict on Kingdom service is this, "As the Father has sent me, even so I send you" (John 20:21). "He who believes in me will also do the works that I do; and greater works than these will he do, because I go to the Father" (John 14:12).

That's what the apostles did. They proclaimed His Word with power. Peter preached on the day of Pentecost and 3,000 people were converted. A man once said to a group of fellow pastors, "Brethren, we need this kind of power. Peter preached one sermon and added 3,000 converts. I have preached more than 3,000 sermons and I sometimes wonder if I have had one real convert!"

And the apostles did miracles! They healed the sick, they cast out demons, they loosed people from sin, they taught with authority. Everything they did depended upon the power of the Holy Spirit. That is what Jesus had done.

Again the old Pretender picks up his eight-word assault and says, "*Let me tell you what I can do.* Miracles and things like that back in the Bible is one thing, but we have to be reasonable, practical." This is another Pretender that

God has been dealing with down through the history of the church, and He is dealing with it decisively in our own day. He's dealing with this Pretender who has appointed human reason as his chief counselor and the philosophy of naturalism as his final judge.

I once wrote a paper on a leading theologian. In his writings he said that "modern man" can't believe in miracles and things supernatural. The gospel must be reshaped so that it will be acceptable and understandable to "modern man." Then I became a pastor and I bumped into a whole bunch of "modern men" right in the congregation, because our church is in a commuting community for the aerospace industry. These scientists and engineers are the kind of people this theologian meant by "modern man"—men who put the Apollo on the moon, design space shuttles, develop laser-beam technology. And I found that they didn't have as much trouble with miracles as theologians do. They pray for the sick. They exercise spiritual gifts. They take seriously the promises of God. It's only a prejudiced, limited reason that rules out the supernatural.

The Spirit is causing people to break loose from the thrall of this Pretender and once again to acknowledge the Rightful King, who is a God of miracles. The gifts of the Holy Spirit are tools of the Rightful King, which His servants use in carrying out His gracious rule among His people. They are working today!

When the issue is our ministry, we have to quit telling God what *we* cannot or can do, and let Him tell us what *He* is planning to do, and that is to carry out the ministry of Jesus through His body, the church.

We have to be continually alert to the attempts of the Pretender to *rob Christ of His glory* by getting us to water down our expectations of this great King to the level of human possibility. We need to feel that sharp point of the sword of the Spirit at our throats. This is a life-and-death struggle, and the only thing I can do when the sword of the Spirit presses against my "flesh" is surrender. "Lord, I give up! I'm going to quit telling you what *I* can do, because it's finally beginning to get through to me that that's not what the Christian life is all about. It's not what I can do; it's what you are going to do in this ministry that makes the difference. What are you going to do by the power of your Spirit? That's what I want to be involved in. Lord, I give up my assault upon the throne of Christ. Let King Jesus, the Rightful king, be upon the throne. Let Him tell me what He's going to do."

What does He do? He calls me to a ministry of undiluted, unshackled faith in Him.

This God who calls us to receive unmerited grace, this God who calls us to unconditional obedience, also promises us unlimited power to carry out the ministry to which He calls us.

Chapter 10

The House with Many Doors

One summer my daughter and some of her friends went "house-sitting" for people who were on vacation. I mused about that one afternoon and it reminded me of our life as Christians. Becoming a Christian is something like moving into a new house. We enter a whole new set of spiritual surroundings.

But we soon discover that the house doesn't really belong to us. The owner maintains possession. As I thought about this a little poem came to me—

HOUSE-SITTING

I live in a house with many doors,
With hallways and windows and seventeen floors;
There's a game room, a library, and a furnace, I think,
And bathrooms and bedrooms in three shades of pink.

There's more to this house than I have explored
(Quite frankly, it's more than I could afford.)
But it doesn't belong to me, you see,
I'm only house-sitting—I live here for free.

When I first moved in, Oh! what a blast.
Never entered my head that it wouldn't last.
I slid down the banisters and ran up the stairs,
I sang in the showers and I lounged in the chairs.

About a month or so later, I forget just when,
Came a knock on a side door about a quarter to ten;

I answered the knock, though I had other things planned,
And there stood the owner with an empty sack in
   his hand.

"It's the garbage," he said, without blinking an eye.
"It's past time we got it; it's piled sky-high."
Now I thought I had hidden it, made it look real nice,
But he went straight to it without looking twice.

The next day he knocked on a door out back
And said, "Let's take a run on the high school track."
Well, I puffed and I panted till my lungs should burst
And the blisters on my feet—they were the worst!

A week or so later, when the sun was down,
He came on by—it must have been with half the town.
"Let's cook a barbeque," he said.
"The folks are hungry, they haven't been fed."

Well, he keeps coming back, this owner does.
This house-sitting isn't all that I thought it was.
In fact, I get the distinct impression
That he intends to maintain possession.

He doesn't turn it over to do as I please,
Seems he's got some of his own ideas.
He's friendly and kind and he doesn't get mad.
He just keeps saying, "You'll get the hang of it, lad.

"This house you're sitting is a special creation,
I designed it for you and I call it 'Salvation.'
But it's more than a matter of just moving in,
It's living and growing and conquering sin.

"It's answering the door when I come and knock,
It's removing every hindrance and every block;
It's finding the handle for all the doors;
It's learning to live on seventeen floors!"

In Revelation 3:20 Jesus says, "Behold, I stand at the door and knock; if anyone hears my voice and opens the door, I will come in." It's interesting that this it not spoken to unbelievers but to believers who have grown lukewarm.

The knocking is for those who have already moved into the household of faith.

Imagine that this house we move into when we become Christians is a house with many doors. The doors represent different ways or places that Jesus seeks to gain fresh access to our lives. We experience renewal—we come to a greater measure of wholeness—as we respond to His knocking.

1. *Doors on the Other Side of the House*

These are truths and ways of doing things that are not only different but are actually contradictory to our usual way of thinking and living. Part of Christ's program to make us whole comes through those doors on the other side of the house. In practical terms this means that we must come to recognize and appreciate *the paradoxical nature of biblical truth.*

What does this mean? God's truth is too big, too heavenly for my little human mind to encompass. It is like a ring ten miles in diameter and my brain is two inches by four inches. How can God's truth ever get into my little brain? Imagine God snipping that perfect ring at one point, then taking the two ends and feeding them into my mind in two parallel lines. That is the way God's truth comes to me, as a series of opposites or paradoxes. The Bible is full of them.

"Enter not into judgment with thy servant; for no man living is righteous before thee" (Ps. 143:2). "Judge me, O Lord, according to my righteousness and according to the integrity that is in me" (Ps. 7:8).

The skeptics say, "Of course, what do you expect? The Bible was written by all sorts of different people and they simply contradict each other." But that overlooks the fact that the paradoxes of Scripture go deeper than any supposed disagreements between different writers. They are woven right into the texture of divine truth. In Proverbs 26, for instance, the paradox comes in two successive verses: "Answer *not* a fool according to his folly, lest you be like him yourself [v. 4]. *Answer* a fool according to his folly, lest he be wise in his own eyes [v 5])."

In 1 John 1:8 we read, "If we say we have no sin, we deceive ourselves, and the truth is not in us." Yet later on the same writer says, "No one born of God commits sin" (1 John 3:9).

If you run into one of those people who tries to avoid all the difficult passages of the Bible by saying, "I only accept the words of Jesus," try this one on him:

"He who is not with me is against me" (Luke 11:23). "He who is not against us is for us" (Mark 9:40).

Paradoxes are not embarrassing intrusions into an otherwise error-free Bible, things we must try to explain away somehow. Paradoxes belong to the very nature of biblical truth, and we can never come to maturity as individuals or as bodies of believers until we learn how to handle the paradoxes of Scripture.

What is the solution to a paradox? Consider a practical example. Here are two familiar sayings: "Look before you leap"; "He who hesitates is lost."

Which one is true? Well, they are both true. But they are not both equally true in every situation. If you are a lone scout with the Arizona 7th Cavalry and Geronimo and his men are in hot pursuit, and you come to a high cliff overlooking a river, and the Indians are two minutes behind you, your truth is, "He who hesitates is lost!" Jump—and pray for deep water!

But if they are half an hour behind, then your truth might well be, "Look before you leap." Scout along the river. Maybe you can find a place to ford, even cover up your trail.

A paradox is not solved by mental contortions that try to "harmonize" the contradictions. A paradox is solved in time, in history, in experience. It is solved by a rhythm that moves from one pole of the paradox to the other according to the wisdom which the Lord gives in each circumstance.

In Exodus 14:14 Moses says to the people of Israel who

were being pursued by the Egyptians, "The Lord will fight for you and you have only to be still." He remembered the fearful plagues God had sent on the Egyptians and he was ready to sit back and watch God do it again. But in the very next verse the Lord says, "Why do you cry to me? Tell the people of Israel to go forward!"

It is not enough to ask, "Is this word scriptural, is it true?" We also have to ask, "Is it the word the Spirit is giving us in this situation? *Is it God's 'now' word?*"

> For everything there is a season, and a time for
>   every matter under heaven:
> A time to be born and a time to die;
> A time to plant, and a time to pluck up what is planted;
> A time to kill, and a time to heal;
> A time to break down, and a time to build up;
> A time to weep, and a time to laugh;
> A time to mourn, and a time to dance;
> A time to cast away stones, and a time to gather
>   stones together;
> A time to embrace, and a time to refrain from
>   embracing;
> A time to seek, and a time to lose;
> A time to rend, and a time to sew;
> A time to keep silence, and a time to speak;
> A time to love, and a time to hate;
> A time for war, and a time for peace. (Eccles. 3:1-8)

Matthew Arnold once said, "There is nothing so irresistible as an idea whose time has come." That is doubly true when the idea is a word of the living God, a word He has designated for this particular time and place, His "now" word.

We sometimes flatter ourselves by thinking that a truth we hold dearly is something that we have discovered, whereas it is much more the case that the truth has discovered us in a particular time and place. Aleksandr Solzhenitsyn has written, "Even the most open-minded among us can only embrace that part of the truth into which his own snout has blundered." That, I believe, is a much more humble and accurate assessment of how we come into truth.

One of the problems God has with His church is that she has memorized His yesterday-words so well and chants them so loudly that she doesn't hear that gentle knock when it comes on the other side of the house, where Christ is standing with a today-word.

A young seminary student asked me to read a paper he had written for one of his classes. In the paper he evaluated a particular education program in which young people not only had classes and Bible studies but also took on a practical service project. He commented, "This would help children realize that being a Christian is not merely knowing the doctrines of the church; it is helping other people in concrete ways." Then he made this interesting observation in the paper: "This past semester I heard so much about 'grace' that I am getting tired of hearing that word. We need to understand the beauty of God's grace, but if it is mentioned too much it becomes a shallow and lifeless word. Works are a needed aspect of the Christian life, for without them faith is dead."

For many Protestants that's a door on the other side of the house. The door on their side says, "By works of the law shall no one be justified" (Gal. 2:16). But the door on the other side of the house says, "You see that a man is justified by works and not by faith alone" (James 2:24).

Today Jesus is knocking at this door on the other side of the house. If you hang around with people who have answered that knock, you hear words like "obedience" and "lordship." *The lordship of Christ*—that's what the Spirit is talking about over on that side of the house.

Why? Why is the Spirit bringing this emphasis on practical obedience and the lordship of Christ? Because Christians have been dispensing too much of what Dietrich Bonhoeffer called "cheap grace." Just believe in Jesus. It's all free. No obligation. No discipleship. No trouble. No demands. No suffering. Smorgasbord Christianity. Take what you like and leave what you don't like.

So Jesus has gone around to the other side of the house and knocked—looking for people who are willing to listen seriously not only to His promises as Savior, but to His claims as Lord. The "lordship of Christ" is a today-word.

Why does Christ come knocking at doors on the other side of the house? He wants to BALANCE what has become one-sided.

2. One-Way Doors That Open Only Out

These are doors where the world comes knocking—the world with its words, its values, its claims. They are designed so we can go out into the world, but we are not to let the world come in and shape the life-style of God's people.

Jesus said, "You are in the world, but not of the world." The world is the arena in which you live out your life, but the world is not the source from which your life flows. In practical terms that means that you don't let the world come in and fill up the house with its words, its values, its way of doing things.

There are door-to-door salesmen that come knocking on these one-way doors, trying to get us to open up so they can slip in and peddle their phony wares, such as:

J. Instant Quick. "Good morning, sir, Glad to find you home. Allow me to introduce myself: J. Instant Quick. If you'll just open the door so I can slip in, I have something here that I think will interest you. It's a wait-reduction pill. My own secret formula. No, no, my friend. It has nothing to do with dieting. It's the other kind of wait—W-A-I-T.

"Now you know as well as I do how frustrating it can be to have to wait for something that you really want. And J. Instant Quick says, 'Why wait?' One of my little wait-reduction pills will dissolve every restraint, every inhibition, every foolish notion that you need to discipline your appetites and desires. With J. Instant Quick wait-reduction pills, when you want something, when you feel something, you do it *right now*!

"Who's buying them? Why everybody's buying them! Last month I sold a whole case to a group of young couples in Minneapolis. Some preacher up there had said that the greatest danger America faces is the fact that children are no longer cherished; young people are turning away from the responsibilities of marriage and parenthood. Well, once these young couples took my wait-reduction pills they easily brushed that kind of talk aside. After all, why let marriage or children stand in the way of doing what you want when you want to?

"And the kids are buying my pills by the bushel. High school and college kids are some of my best customers. Believe me, they sit up and take notice when J. Instant Quick says, 'Why wait? What you want you can have—now!'

"Churches are one of my best growth accounts. I've got a whole pile of testimonials from individuals and churches that have gotten freed up for things like trial marriages, easy divorce, abortion—that whole bag.

"Of course you know there's this whole thing about Christianity being a business of patient endurance. But let a church go through a few struggles chewing on that and they're ready to have J. Instant Quick point out a few short-cuts for handling things like falling membership, financial difficulties, critics, trouble-makers, theological controversy—you name it.

"And people who want to be more spiritual buy from me, too. Fact of the matter is, what you desire can be as high as heaven or as low as hell—J. Instant Quick has a wait-reduction pill made to order just for you."

Covet O'Drool. "How do you do, ma'am. I hope I may have a few moments of your time. I'm Covet O'Drool, representative of the world's largest manufacturer of see-sick pills. You don't need any? You're not planning a voyage? Well, that's a mistake many people make when they first hear about our product. But, you see, it's not that kind of 'sea.' These are *see*-sick pills—S-E-E.

"Let me ask you, have you ever seen something you'd

like to have but—well, you thought you shouldn't have it, or couldn't afford it, or it might even be wrong for you to have it? Ever feel that way? Of course you have; we all do from time to time. Well, now, when you take one of our see-sick pills, you don't just look at that thing and then forget about it. Oh, no! With one of our pills in you, when you see that thing you get sick, positively sick, until you can get your hands on it. What you see and want, you just have to have.

"And take a tip from Covet O'Drool: When you get really see-sick—when you want what you see badly enough—you'll find a way to get it.

"Of course we do a brisk business in the publicity items like murder, robbery, adultery, and so on. But over-all those are low-volume specialty items. Our big volume is house-to-house in neighborhoods just like your own. It's for everyday things like impulse items at the supermarket; or a bigger car, bigger house, bank account, extra clothes; or intangible things like recognition, position, popularity.

"I had a good sale going in a charismatic prayer group a few months back. About six of the people had their eye on the leadership of the group. All six were taking our pills, so there was more jockeying than a Kentucky Derby until they finally broke up into three groups. That cut back my sales, of course, but it opened my eyes to this religious market. Let me tell you, when religious people get see-sick, they go after what they want like nothing you've ever seen. What makes it rugged, of course, is that they do it all in the name of the Lord so some people don't even realize they're see-sick. Sometimes I wonder whether they know it themselves.

"Well, no matter. It's all one to Covet O'Drool. Our pills cover the whole nine yards. Whatever you set your eye on, our pills will make you so see-sick that you'll go after it with never a worry about what happens to other people."

I. Magnum Big. "Good evening, my friend. I hope you have a few moments for your friendly I-glass salesman, I.

Magnum Big. That's me, I. Magnum Big, and I handle the world's most complete line of I-glasses. You say you don't need glasses, have 20-20 vision? Splendid! All the more reason for you to be interested in my product. You see, I don't carry the kind of glasses you fit on your face to correct your vision. Mine are glasses you drink out of. *I*-glasses, capital 'I' you know, as in, 'I am happy,' or, 'I am my own boss.'

"Let me ask you, have you ever wanted to be your own boss? Have you ever gotten sick and tired of always having to answer to someone else? Of course you have! And you can be your own boss. You see, with every I-glass we give you get an appropriate dosage of I-glass powder-mix. Just add water, drink it down while it's still foaming, and your 'I,' that is, your self—your own unique, distinctive, winsome personality—declares its independence.

"Now we have all sizes and shapes of I-glasses. You may want to start out with a little one-swallow glass and get free from a bothersome neighbor. We have bigger glasses for relatives and family. Of course we have group-glasses for handling almost any kind of controversy. And it doesn't matter whether you put them out or they put you out, our I-glasses work on both ends of the stick. The main thing is to end up independent—no ties, no more irritating adjustments and compromises, no one telling you or your group what to do or how to act.

"My friend, when you drink from one of our I-glasses, you savor the essence of life itself. And with each and every purchase you get a free handkerchief embossed with the personal motto of I. Magnum Big: 'Like Adam and Eve, I want to be free; I don't need you, and you don't need me.' "

You no doubt recognize these three peddlers of the world's wisdom. The apostle John calls them the *lust of the flesh*, the *lust of the eyes*, and *pride of life*. (See I John 2:15-16.) He says we shouldn't have anything to do with them. These are one-way doors where they come knocking—doors we should keep tightly closed against a world that wants to come and sell us its life-style.

Why does Christ caution us against opening the door to the world's influence? He wants to PROTECT what is endangered.

3. Boarded-Up Doors

These doors represent neglected truths, sometimes embattled truths that we would rather not recognize.

The charismatic renewal shows us a good example of Jesus knocking at some boarded-up doors: healing, tongues, prophecy, vision, revelation. These spiritual gifts are not the whole of the renewal, by any means. But they are doors where Christ has come knocking.

The charismatic renewal has often been challenged by church leaders and theologians: "Why this emphasis on spiritual gifts, especially speaking in tongues? We had great spiritual revivals in the past without them. Why are they necessary?"

That kind of question approaches spiritual renewal as though it were a formula we could manipulate to suit ourselves. But spiritual renewal is initiated by the Lord. He comes knocking at the door. Renewal takes place when we open the door where He is knocking.

I'm interested to learn about doors He's knocked at in times past. That's part of my education and heritage as a believer. But I am vitally concerned—my spiritual health depends upon—learning where He is knocking *today* and responding to that knock.

"Couldn't we have spiritual renewal just as well without the gifts?" My answer would be, "No, I do not believe so." Not because it is not theoretically possible; Christ is free to renew His church any way He chooses. But Christ has chosen in our day to lay particular emphasis on the work of the Holy Spirit and the operation of spiritual gifts.

The course of the Pentecostal and charismatic movements indicates that He has sovereignly chosen to use the gift of speaking in tongues in a special way as a kind of catalyst for renewal. It may not make sense to our human reason. We might put our theological brains together and imagine better ways He might have done it. But the Lord Christ does not accommodate His ways to our thinking. He comes knocking where He chooses. He has come in our day to a church often puffed up with a sense of her own wisdom and learning and said, "Will you open to me here? Will you open up this 'least of the gifts' that has been boarded up so long?"

Church leaders and theologians have often looked upon spiritual gifts as though charismatics had chosen them on their own initiative. If that were the case, this renewal movement would not be sweeping the earth as it is today. It has not been a matter of people simply choosing these gifts. The Lord Jesus has chosen to come knocking at these doors and people have responded to His knocking. The controversy, if there be one, is not with charismatics, but with the Lord. The issue is not spiritual gifts. *The issue is the lordship of Christ.* This is His work, His initiative, His renewal. He will welcome people into it, including theologians, but He will not account to them for it, nor trim it to fit their theological prescriptions. He is Lord to do in His church as He pleases. And if He chooses, in His sovereign wisdom— the wisdom that makes foolishness of man's wisdom—to draw a battle line over even such a seemingly little thing as speaking in tongues, then that is the place where one dare not scoff but rather must take his stand.

Martin Luther once said, "If I profess with the loudest voice and clearest exposition every portion of the truth of God except precisely that little point which the world and the devil are at that moment attacking, I am not confessing Christ, however boldly I may be professing Christ. Where the battle rages there the loyalty of the soldier is proved, and to be steady on all the battle front besides is mere flight and disgrace if he flinches at this point."

Why does Christ come knocking at boarded-up doors?
He wants to RESTORE what has been neglected.

4. *French Doors*

These are windowed doors that look out on the garden, and beyond that to the street, where all sorts of "other people" are milling around. Now it's one thing to look out at them through the glass, while you are safely separated. Oh, you may have some high-level dialogues and consultations, but what happens when Jesus knocks at the French Doors and you find out He's going to bring them right into the house?

The Lord does not bring renewal to prop up and bless the status quo. He brings it to advance His program, which is to make His followers one, as He and the Father are one. Those who think that a work of God can be manipulated and used to further their own plans will find their house growing silent. Oh, they can ignore the Lord's knocking, slide shut the bolt on the French Doors, and try to have a nice, safe, domesticated renewal in their own living rooms, but then the knocking will grow silent on the other doors too. And soon they will be living with only the memory of a renewal that once was.

Just as we need one another as individuals in a local church, we need each other as different traditions and denominations in the church universal. How do we discern where the Lord is knocking? If we go purely on our own understanding of Scripture and our own guidance, we are likely to go off on a tangent. The Bible says that the prophetic word must be weighed and tested in the body of believers (1 Cor. 14:29). The Lord comes knocking at the French Doors because He wants the different branches of His scattered family to begin to help and counsel with one another. He wants us to encourage, assist, admonish and correct one another. He wants us to hear and respond to the fullness of His today-word, and in order to do that we need each other.

Why does Christ come knocking at the French Doors? He wants to RECONCILE what is separated.

5. *The Door with the Smooth Doorknob*

This door represents the traditional way of understanding and living the Christian life in our particular church. The doorknob has been worn smooth by much use. This door is the Catholic's regard for church order, the Wesleyan's emphasis on holiness, the Lutheran's justification by faith, the Pentecostal's baptism with the Holy Spirit. It is the aspect of God's revelation which has had particular significance for some part of God's family.

It is important that we learn to honor the wisdom that the church has gained through the centuries. Renewal movements that do not cultivate an appreciation of history rob themselves of many treasures that God has entrusted to the church, and they almost certainly doom themselves to repeating mistakes that history could have warned them about.

Back in the early 1960's Donald Gee, the Pentecostal patriarch of Great Britain, wrote an open letter to "our new Pentecostal friends" who were then just beginning to spring up in the historic Protestant denominations. He cautioned them not to abandon their scholarly study of Scripture or theological training. In the enthusiasm and excitement of a fresh outpouring of the Spirit it is a temptation to emphasize experience at the expense of a serious study of the Word and theological reflection. That is a lesson from history that leaders in any renewal movement would be wise to heed.

On the other hand, church officials need to keep their ears open for the knock of the Lord that comes at some other door than this one with the smooth doorknob. It is one thing to weigh with sober judgment to see whether a thing be of God, but too often church leaders and theologians react to a fresh breeze of the Spirit like irritable old codgers disturbed at their intellectual chess games by a pack of unruly children. Periodically they unbutton their starched collars, roll up their French cuffs, and storm outside to conduct investigations, proving that they have the one really authentic door through which Jesus comes. His footprints are still in the dust outside. His fingerprints are on the door knocker. And one of the rose bushes caught a thread of His robe as He passed by, proving beyond the shadow of a doubt that He was right here at this very door—in 1517, and 1743, and 1901. . . .

I am grateful for the yesterday-words of God. I am grateful for the people who responded to those words, who opened a door and let Jesus in. I am grateful for St. Benedict, and Francis, and Luther, and Calvin, and Wesley, and Moody. But no generation can be renewed simply by rehearsing how people responded to God in days gone by. Where is the Lord knocking now? What word out of His storehouse of truth is He laying particular emphasis on today?

This is not to say that truth changes from day to day or from generation to generation—"situational doctrine" to match "situational ethics." God's truth is eternal and unchanging. But according to where we are in our journey toward wholeness, the Spirit will accent a particular aspect of God's truth that we need right now.

If we have worn the doorknob smooth on one particular door, we can pretty well expect a knock at some other door to bring us into better balance. It doesn't mean that we abandon the door with the smooth doorknob and the truth that it represents. It just means that we are humble enough to recognize that we don't have a monopoly on the truth, and that in heeding the Lord's knock at another door we are not abandoning the truth; rather, we are honoring Christ's sovereign lordship and allowing Him to bring us to a greater measure of wholeness.

Why does Christ go beyond the smooth doorknob? He wants to BUILD UPON what has been given.

6. *Garage Doors*

These are doors through which we move out into the

world in groups and under power. This is no ordinary garage. It is an underground staging area for an army.

Jesus said, "The gates of hell shall not prevail against my church" (Matt. 16:18). That is a picture of a church engaged in spiritual warfare. Jesus brings His church to wholeness for himself that she might be His spotless Bride. But another image close to that of the Bride is the image of the Lord's people as an army—"Who is this that looks forth like the dawn, fair as the moon, bright as the sun, terrible as an army with banners?" (Song of Sol. 6:10)—the Army, the Bridal Army.

The Lord brings His people to wholeness that they might march at His side in the day of battle and bring down the strongholds of the enemy.

When Jesus swings open the garage doors He wants a people who can move out in rank and order, at His command. He wants a people who have learned to deny self in order to serve the body—not only at the personal level, but also at the level of the group, congregation, denomination. He wants a people who have moved beyond personal deliverance to disciplined obedience, beyond blessing to battle-readiness. God is readying His people for battle.

A group of us were once traveling in Israel. One man in the group made a simple observation that revealed very accurately an important aspect of God's battle strategy in our day.

We were passing by one of the many *kibbutzim* that dot that tiny land. Each kibbutz is a small, disciplined, and highly dedicated community that is both a thriving center of life and production, and also helps form the country's first line of defense.

This brother made the observation that the history of Israel offers many parallels to the life and history of the church. The kibbutz is an illustration of one of the significant things that God is doing in our day. Throughout christendom God is raising up committed, dedicated bodies of believers. It is not a new denomination. It is a network of outposts strategically placed throughout the world, thriving centers of life but having a level of dedication, selflessness, and discipline that the Lord can count on in a special way in the day of battle.

The form and style of these bodies is varied, as are the kibbutzim in Israel. You may find one of these outposts in a nondenominational fellowship, or an Episcopal parish, or a mission station, or an ecumenical community, or a Baptist or Lutheran congregation. They are not linked organizationally, but they share a common sense of the Lord's purpose and moving in our day.

These outposts do not exist for themselves but for the sake of the whole people. We learned that Israelis who live in the kibbutzim number less than three percent of the population. Yet they have contributed more than fifty percent of the nation's leaders, and more than twenty-five percent of her wartime casualties.

In this and many other ways the Lord is preparing His people for battle. The tide of evil is rising. The spiritual hosts of wickedness are massing their forces in awesome array. If we did not know that the Lord is also working out His strategy, our hearts would fail us for fear. But *He* is at work. Quietly He is going throughout the length and breadth of the land, knocking, knocking, knocking—seeking fresh access to the lives of His people that He might come in and build them into himself as a Bridal Army.

Why does the Lord open the garage doors and lead forth His people? He wants to UNITE all things in Christ.

> We live in a house with many doors
> With brothers and sisters on seventeen floors;
> Now that's quite a family, you'll have to admit,
> There's nothing on earth to compare with it.
> When you first move in it's all pretty new.
> You'll have some getting acquainted to do;
> But don't let it throw you, you've nothing to fear;
> Just remember, the Lord is always here.
>
> Well, yes, we are house-sitting, in a way that's true;
> Though it's not like you'd think, for He's here with you;
> But He's so loving and humble (It's a wonder to me);
> He always knocks, and asks, "Are you . . . free?"

Chapter 11

Private Confession

"Confess your sins to one another, and pray for one another, that you may be healed" (James 5:16).

If you were to go to a newsstand, pick up a number of magazines at random and leaf through the Tables of Contents, more than likely you'd run across several articles dealing with some sort of human problem—and offering some sort of solution. The problems might vary from strife in the community, to family problems, to deep personal insecurity; the solutions might vary from changing your diet, to a new way of thinking, to some kind of social readjustment, to a reevaluation of your career . . . and so on.

The Bible's Diagnosis of Human Problems

In the face of these kinds of solutions to human problems, the word of the Bible seems frightfully simple. The Bible diagnoses our human problems with one simple word: *sin*. Our first need as human beings is not security or understanding or social adjustment or peace of mind or anything else. The need we have which underlies every other need is a solution to the problem of sin.

Imagine a doctor trained at the UCLA Medical Center. When he has finished his training, he goes out to a remote uncivilized area. In the village where he sets up practice, a man is stricken with labored breathing and a heavy congestion of the chest.

The local medicine man says an evil spirit is trying to get out of him; they should let some of his blood so the spirit can get out. Some of the women of the village whisper that he built his hut too close to the edge of the forest and the forest gods are attacking him. His mother and several elderly aunts come by and tell him that it must be his wife who is the cause of his sickness because she hasn't borne him any male children; he had better get rid of his wife and take another. But when the doctor comes to examine him, he brushes aside all of these diagnoses. The man has acute pneumonia. There is an infection inside him which must be dealt with and then he will get well. The doctor administers the proper drugs to him and starts him on the road back to health.

There are a lot of medicine-man theories and old wives' tales going around in our day as to what is really wrong with the human race. They have one great error in common: Like the natives in our illustration, they are looking for the cause of man's trouble somewhere outside of man himself. It's his environment, or his family, or he's in the wrong job, or his parents didn't understand him, or society is too competitive, and on and on. The Bible brushes all of these diagnoses aside. Man is a sinner. He has a deadly spiritual sickness inside him that must be dealt with and then he will get well. You can change every one of his outward circumstances and it won't help him one bit unless the problem of his sin is dealt with at the very root.

It seems we have to relearn this truth every so often. When problems mount up we begin to slip off to consult the "witch doctors," so the Lord has to dispatch us back to Square 1 where we take another long, serious look at the problem of sin.

The doctor in our illustration not only correctly diagnosed the sickness, he took steps to cure it. He administered healing drugs personally and directly to the sick man. It isn't enough that we agree with the doctrine that man is a sinner. It isn't enough to come together in church and repeat in unison a general confession. This is like a man whose doctor tells him he has a dangerous heart condition; the man nods and agrees—he accepts the diagnosis. But when the doctor tells him that therefore he must go on a strict diet, curtail his business activities and stop smoking, the man shrugs and walks away. It didn't help him to accept the diagnosis because he didn't follow through on the personal application. Diagnosis is only helpful when it leads to a practical application.

The Bible's Prescription

James 5:16 gives a practical prescription for effectively dealing wih sin. The prescription reads: "Confess your sins to one another"—private and personal confession of your sins to another person.

"Private confession? I don't need to confess my sins to another person! I can confess them directly to God!"

I know the questions and objections. I remember how they rose up in my mind when this scripture was first pointed out to me. But after I had made all my arguments and came back, this text was quietly standing there: "Confess your sins to one another."

It's part of our human nature to defend ourselves against a new truth, especially if it makes us somewhat uncomfortable on first impact. Though the idea of actually confessing my sins to another person was quite a threatening idea when I first began to consider it, I pondered this matter for quite a time. The Lord was gentle and patient with me. Every so often He would seem to bring me to some person or article or book that would say a favorable word about the practice of private confession.

Of course, the first line of defense for a Protestant is usually, "Oh, that's just something Catholic!" I was raised in a strong Lutheran community where we did not have much to do with Catholics. (I heard of one girl in our town who came through confirmation instruction with the settled idea that at the end of the world there was going to be a big war between the Catholics and the Lutherans, and the winners would go to heaven!) One of the devil's cheapest, yet most effective, tricks is to paste an unfavorable or mysterious label on truth to keep us from investigating it with an open mind. It is true, of course, that private confession is practiced in the Roman and Greek Catholic churches. But so are the Lord's Supper, and prayer, and worship of God.

When I got over the barrier of that label, I discovered that private confession wasn't so exclusively Catholic as I had thought. In fact, I found out that it had deep roots in my own Lutheran church. In our Lutheran Catechism, right between the teaching on Baptism and the teaching on the Lord's Supper, there is a little section giving instructions for making private confession. Martin Luther himself practiced private confession all his life and said of it, "No one will ever rob me of the privilege of private confession; it is the greatest comfort to my soul."

When we go into church history we discover that private confession was practiced outside the Catholic church up until the end of the 18th century—200 years after Luther. So it was not the Reformation that let the practice of private confession slip away. It slipped away during the Age of Rationalism—a movement that led droves of people away from a biblical faith and whose bitter fruit we are still reaping today.

"Confess your sins to one another. . . . " When I looked at it objectively, I realized that private confession was very much a part of my own tradition, even though it was not widely practiced and I had never personally made use of it. After some of my questions had been answered along this line, the Lord seemed to keep bringing me the witness of people who spoke favorably about the practice of private confession.

For instance, a professor whom I very much respected at the seminary wrote an article entitled, "Private Confession or Psychoanalysis." The theme of his article was simply this: If the church does not make available to her people the confessional, they will be driven to the psychiatrist's couch by the burden of unconfessed sin.

Some years ago the prayer groups in our church read *The Healing Light* by Agnes Sanford. She related many experiences in prayer, especially prayer for the sick. But she came to a time when her prayers seemed to have no more power. She was spiritually exhausted. She couldn't understand what had gone wrong until a friend pointed her to the practice of private confession. She took the advice, went to a minister of her church, made a complete confession—and found that her power in prayer was restored.

In Germany there is a group called the "Marburg Circle," which has led thousands of people to a personal and vital faith in Christ. One of their key emphases is the practice of private confession. When I first heard some of these people witness of their faith in Christ—and very often mention that faith had suddenly become real during that hour of confession—I knew that they had touched on a deep spiritual truth.

There came a time in my own experience when the Lord seemed to tell me, "Be a doer of the word, and not a hearer only, deceiving yourself" (James 1:22). It scared me. What would someone think of me if I went to him and confessed all my sins?

The Lord graciously led me to a professor at the seminary (I was a student at the time) with a warm heart and much pastoral experience. We met together one day and I made confession. I had prepared it over a period of about a week and written down the things to be confessed.

Ever since that day, the word "forgiveness" has had a whole new meaning for me. It had often been only an intellectual concept; now it had become a living reality. I have gone to private confession from time to time since then, and have always found in it a special blessing.

Theoretically you can confess your sins directly to God, and receive His forgiveness. But there are times and situations where the theory doesn't work out in practice. This must be so, or else this text would never have been given us in the Bible. God puts no idle words in Scripture—everything there has a definite purpose. This word, "Confess your sins to one another," is given to us because we sometimes need the help of private confession to "spring loose" a sin so we can actually be freed from its power and its accusation.

There is a need to be specific about our sins. The general confession that "I am a sinner—all men are sinners" can actually cover up specific sins. We may make this kind of a general confession every Sunday in church. Yet if a neighbor calls to our attention some specific sin, how quick we are to deny it, to defend ourselves! We need to look at our sins, name them one by one—seeking forgiveness for things we can specifically point to in our own life.

A vow of *absolute confidentiality* stands over the confessional. A priest or pastor is under obligation never to reveal anything which is told him in confession. This vow is even respected in court. If a pastor were ever called upon to testify in court, he could not be forced to reveal anything told him in the privacy of confession.

Private confession affords the special blessing of personal absolution. Having confessed your sins, you hear with your own ears the word that assures you of God's forgiveness. God knows the weakness of our human nature. He knows that there are times when we need to receive the assurance of forgiveness in a special and personal way. He has given to His church this special authority, "If you forgive the sins of any, they are forgiven!" (John 20:23). The exercise of this power is particularly effective and appropriate in connection with private confession.

What is the promise of God in regard to private confession? Scripture links it with the promise of power—power in prayer. Confession dredges out the channel of prayer so the power of God can flow through it with greater effectiveness. It is no coincidence that every great revival is preceded by seasons of deep confession among God's people.

A Practical Guide to Private Confession

"What is Confession? Confession consists of two parts: the one is that we confess our sins; the other, that we receive absolution or forgiveness from the Pastor as from God himself, in no wise doubting, but firmly believing, that our sins are thereby forgiven before God in heaven."—Martin Luther.

Counseling and Confession

Many people confuse counseling with confession. The purpose of counseling is to help you understand and interpret your sins, failures, frustrations. The purpose of confession is simply to admit them—without explanation or alibi—before God, yourself, and another person.

For example, if you have trouble with a sharp temper and you come for counseling, you would explain your background and situation, and the circumstances in which you lose your temper. In time a counselor could perhaps help you to better understand and control your temper. But if you came for confession, you would simply admit, without explanation or alibi, that on such-and-such occasions you lost your temper and spoke unkindly, that you earnestly repent of that sin, desire God's forgiveness, and pray that by His grace and power He will work an even temper in you.

The aim of counseling is to gain understanding so you can better deal with your problem. The aim of confession is to gain forgiveness so God can deal with your problem. Both have their place but they should not be confused.

Confession, therefore, is a means God has given to help you obtain the full blessing of His forgiveness. It is a humble admission to God, to yourself, and to your pastor of every known sin. A heart burdened and weakened by guilt often needs the help of another Christian in order to yield up sin and lay hold on God's forgiveness. That is the reason for confession to your pastor. His presence and silent prayer during your confession helps you let go of your sins and lay them at the foot of the Cross. Then, by speaking to you God's Word, he helps you claim and lay hold on the forgiveness which is yours in Christ. God alone forgives sin. Your pastor is simply there to help you receive that forgiveness. God knows the weakness of our faith in times of sin-burden; therefore He gives us this means to deal with sin more effectively: "Confess your sins to one another."

How to Make a Confession

Key: Begin and end each step in prayer, asking that God will help and guide you—according to your need and His wisdom.

1. Prepare Your Confession

"This is my first confession."

If you have never made a confession before, you can make it for your entire past life. The release and freedom which God gives you will more than repay you for the time and effort of preparing a thorough confession.

The following method, suggested by Agnes Sanford in her book, *The Healing Light*, is simple and effective. Divide your life into 7-year periods. Seven suggests a "circle of completed time" in Scripture and it is a small enough unit to work with fairly easily. Make up a little notebook or folder with a page for every 7-year period in your life, up to the present time.

Set aside a definite time each day to prepare your confession. Ten to fifteen minutes will usually be enough to start with. As you move along into the more recent years of your life you may need more time. Begin each session by praying that the Holy Spirit will help you recall anything which should be confessed. *This is absolutely essential, for only the Holy Spirit can lead us to true repentance.*

Have a paper and pencil at hand as you prepare your confession. The first day you go back to the first seven years of your life. You write down on that sheet anything which should be confessed. The second day you cover the years from 7-14, the third day 14-21, and so on. Naturally you will not have much to write down in the first period. It will increase as you move along. If a memory from, say, your twelfth year stirs up something quite definite and significant from your twentieth year, you may make a note of it on the proper page. But, generally speaking, try to stay in the period you are dealing with on that particular day. You can trust the Holy Spirit to stir your memory when you come to the next period.

"Should I go into much detail for each thing I write down?"

That is not necessary. A note or two will enable you to recall the incident when you come for private confession. In making your confession do only enough explaining so the pastor will know specifically the sin or incident which you are confessing. Avoid any attempt to "explain" or "justify" yourself. God knows all the circumstances involved, and He will not judge you unfairly.

"What sins should I confess? Should I write down anything else besides 'sin'?"

The Marburg Circle suggests four standards to help evaluate one's life: absolute honesty, absolute purity, absolute love, absolute selflessness. These are especially helpful in evaluating your most recent past. Don't mention names or "extenuating circumstances." Your purpose is not to explain, justify, understand, or alibi for your sin, but simply to confess it. Someone has said, "You never lose your peace over someone else's sin, only over your own." If someone has told lies about you and caused you much unhappiness—and you have resented it—simply confess your resentment. Nothing more, nothing less.

In dealing with the more distant past confession has

been called a "healing of the memories." It is not only a confession of sin, in the narrower sense of breaking a commandment; it is also a confession of anything in the past which still causes pain, uneasiness, guilt, hurt, shame when you remember it. This double-aspect of forgiveness is suggested in the hymn, "There is a balm in Gilead to heal the sin-sick soul, there is a balm in Gilead to make the wounded whole." God, our loving heavenly Father, wants to forgive and redeem us from everything which still binds us to our past life—to set us free, wonderfully free, for His future!

2. *Make Your Confession*

Generally speaking it is wise to make your formal confession to a pastor or mature spiritual counselor. Private confession is a sacred trust and cannot be handled lightly.

Briefly mention each sin written down on your paper. As you confess, the pastor stands by you as your "brother in Christ," silently interceding for you. When you have finished he stands before you as God's spokesman, to speak to you the comforting words of God's forgiveness.

Whatever you speak in confession is held in *absolute confidence*. One who receives confession may never reveal what is spoken there.

3. *Leave Your Sins at the Cross*

Satan will try to tell you that God has not really forgiven your sins. He will try to get you to feel guilty all over again. God's Word is stronger than Satan: God has utterly washed away that sin in the blood of Christ; you can forget about it.

Another thing Satan will try to do is to get you to fall into sin again. Resist him, knowing that not only the guilt of that sin but also its power over you has been nailed to the Cross. You can claim, in Christ's name, not only forgiveness but also deliverance. You go forth forgiven and delivered. Claim these benefits in faith—and shortly you will know them in experience.

VI.

The Goal

The goal is not to grow and become something in ourselves,
but continually to return to the place where Christ can
become something in us.

Chapter 12

The Magnificent Paradox

One of the standard objections to the ministry of healing is St. Paul's "thorn in the flesh." The argument goes something like this: St. Paul is a man with impeccable spiritual credentials. St. Paul wasn't healed of his thorn in the flesh. Therefore, healing isn't necessarily the will of God.

The argument warrants a little closer scrutiny. First of all, look carefully at exactly what the apostle says: "Because of the surpassing greatness of the revelations, for this reason, to keep me from exalting myself, there was given me a thorn in the flesh, a messenger of Satan to buffet me—to keep me from exalting myself! Concerning this I entreated the Lord three times that it might depart me. And he has said to me, 'My grace is sufficient for you, for my power is perfected in weakness.' Most gladly, therefore, I will rather boast about my weaknesses, that the power of Christ may dwell in me. Therefore, I am well content with weaknesses, with insults, with distresses, with persecutions, with difficulties, for Christ's sake; for when I am weak, then I am strong" (2 Cor. 12:7-10, ASV).

"Thorn in the flesh" does not necessarily refer to a *physical ailment*. The word "flesh" can mean our basic human nature. Paul is not necessarily talking about something physical at all. Indeed, the thought in this context moves along another line altogether.

He says that the "thorn" was given *to keep him from exalting himself.* Paul had lived through tremendous spiritual experiences: revelations, visions, new tongues, healings, exorcisms. God knew that it would be very easy for these experiences to go to St. Paul's head. A minister once said, "Success in the ministry is strong wine." It would have been easy for Paul to get drunk with a sense of his own success. He could begin to depend upon his own power, his own spirituality, his own resourcefulness in prayer, his own ability in intercession, his own power to cast out demons. He would walk into new mission fields not as he did in Corinth, in fear and trembling, but in boldness and confidence. "Now come and listen to me, you people! I've raised the dead, I've healed the sick, I've cast out spirits. *I'll* tell you the truth about God and Christ. I've got it!" That was a danger, and both Paul and God knew it.

We sometimes think that the sins of the flesh manifest themselves only in telling lies and stealing and cheating and illicit sex. But uncrucified self will even lay hands on the sick, conduct a prayer group, preach the gospel—just as long as he can do it and remain in control.

What the Bible calls "the old man" or the "flesh" may manifest itself in unrighteousness. We all know about that—the sin story. But the flesh will also manifest itself in self-righteousness. For the saved, born-again believer this is by far the greater danger. Agnes Sanford says the greatest danger for the healer is *spiritual pride.*

St. Paul was a yielded instrument. The Lord had worked marvelous things through him. Because of the urgent need, he had given Paul a terrific dose of spiritual experiences. He had to counteract it with a thorn in the flesh—something to nail down Paul's pride in a comatose state so that his power could continue to flow through Paul, to accomplish the work which God wanted to accomplish through him. He wanted to keep him the way he was. Paul understood this, and therefore he said, "Most gladly, therefore, I will rather boast about my weaknesses." He knew that the "thorn" had a purpose: it would keep him effective for the Lord.

Well, then, is Paul's thorn in the flesh supposed to discourage our belief in miracles and healing? Exactly the opposite. God was so concerned about keeping this special channel functioning that He even let the apostle carry a thorn in the flesh in order to keep the channel open and flowing.

We don't know for certain what the "thorn" was, though verse 10 seems to suggest that it was the insults, persecutions, and difficulties which he continually had to undergo for Christ's sake. In any case, it wasn't something irritating just for the sake of being irritating. It had a specific purpose: God wanted to heal him of pride. Let's allow God to use His own methods! Yes, even a thorn in the flesh.

The Paradox: Strength Out of Weakness

This opens up one of the deepest paradoxes of our Christian experience. Paul chisels it out in eight magnificent words: "When I am weak, then I am strong."

Can you image the fullback for the Pittsburgh Steelers making a statement like that? When I am weak, then I am strong. Can you imagine David Rockefeller speaking of the financial condition of the Chase Manhattan Bank with words like that? When I am weak, then I am strong. Ridiculous! They would say, "When I am weak, I am ready for the sidelines, I'm worthless."

But in the spiritual life this is a basic law: When I am weak, then I am strong. This is one of the hardest lessons we have to learn as Christians: we really can't do anything for Christ until we're ready to go to the sidelines, until we see our own efforts and our own self as utterly worthless.

Oh, how the flesh rebels at that! The natural man will do anything to stay in the game. "I'll go to a healing service, I'll give extra money to the church, I'll be there every Sunday singing louder than anybody else. . ."

But the Lord says, "No—the first Adam had his chance." For fifteen hundred years—from Sinai to Calvary—human nature had a chance to prove itself, and it failed—utterly, completely. God said, "You don't need a new insight, or a new religious discipline. You need a *new nature.* And the only way that you're going to get a new nature is if the old nature will move out of the way so that my new nature can come in and take over."

Have you lived this paradox? If you have walked one step with Christ, you've already sensed it: Those times when you feel charged with spiritual power, when you have "all the faith in the world," you fall flat on your face. And when you feel utterly empty and weak, lo and behold, the Lord works through you in a most spectacular way.

I remember the first time I ever called on anyone in a hospital, after I became aware of the ministry of healing. I had just read *The Healing Light* by Agnes Sanford. I went up to this hospital room full of these new ideas and concepts—it was a whole new world that had opened up. And wouldn't you know—I picked the toughest case you could imagine: A tumor in the neck, a woman who had been given a month to live. But that wasn't going to stop me! I was going to lay hands on her and she was going to walk out of that room. . .

We prayed together, and spent many hours together, actually. I tried to explain to her some of my enthusiasm about the ministry of healing. And she did take hold of it. She said it was the only hope that had been given to her. (The Lord sometimes works through us in spite of ourselves!) But one afternoon as I came, I just opened up and said, "You know this is all wonderful—the thought that Jesus really *is* the same yesterday and today and forever. But I just have to confess to you that it is a very humbling experience for me to come to you like this, because when all is said and done I realize that all I come to you with is the simple gospel!" And for the first time in all the times I had visited her, she smiled. "When I am weak, then I am strong." That's probably all the good that my visits did for her—one smile. Somehow or other, when I became weak—

and was ready to face up to it and recognize that I had nothing but the gospel—then the power of the gospel was there. I had been trying to do it with all kinds of new concepts that had been exciting to me, but Jesus was ready to operate through the weakness of the simple gospel.

Spiritual Power: A Potential Danger

The Lord was teaching me a lesson. When I first became aware of the ministry of healing, I latched onto it. I saw the possibility of the power of the New Testament Church coming back into our churches today. But you don't have to be very spiritual to want more power in your Christian life. The flesh is ready any day of the week for more power—as long as it can maintain control of that power.

Wouldn't it be wonderful if you could lay hands on anyone—just anyone at all—and see that person healed? A woman sits down on the bus in the seat ahead of you. You notice that she has a large growth on her neck. You tap her on the shoulder and say, "Dear, the Lord is going to heal you. Just let me touch you there—" And the growth shrinks and disappears right before your eyes! Everybody on the bus shouts, "Glory! Hallelujah! Praise the Lord! Who are you anyway? My, but you're wonderful. Won't you pray with my Uncle John? He has rheumatism so bad. . . ." Then you leave the bus and you see a man on the sidewalk in a wheelchair. You touch him; he stands up and walks away, pushing the chair. Day in and day out, you heal them all. Wouldn't this be wonderful?

Well, it *would* be wonderful. But it doesn't take one bit of spirituality to desire to do that kind of thing. Anybody would love to have that kind of power.

We learn in First Corinthians that the *desire* for spiritual power can be held by people who are carnally minded. We aren't talking here about people living in known sin. These are Christians, but they are still living ninety-eight percent in the flesh and about two percent in the Spirit—

and they want power. It is not a spiritual desire. Desire for power can be a rank desire of the flesh.

The Lord has never worked an instantaneous, miraculous healing through me, so far as I know; and I think I know exactly the reason: I wouldn't be fit to live with. Two days later I'd probably start telling the Lord how to run His business! He let St. Paul off with a thorn in the flesh: He'd have to put me in a straitjacket. The flesh is standing by, ready to corrupt every spiritual blessing the Lord gives us.

The Cross: God's Way of Dealing with the Problem

But the Lord has a marvelous way of dealing with this: Dead men don't grasp; dead men don't corrupt; dead men don't take over. God's solution for the old nature is *death*. He must be given up to death.

Regardless of how God accomplishes this death—whether by a thorn in the flesh as with St. Paul, or by some other means of daily being crucified with Christ—that death to self is an absolute necessity for spiritual growth.

This is the paradox of spiritual living, that when we die we live. Paul says, "When I am weak, then I am strong." Jesus puts it even stronger: "If you die, then you will live." It's a sobering thought—that God's power is blocked, that God's healing power is diminished, because we have not been willing to die to self in order for Christ to live within us.

How do we do this? How do we die to self? In the eleventh chapter of John we find something helpful. When Jesus was going to Jerusalem to His death—which is the type of our dying to self—one of the apostles said, "Let us also go, that we may die with him."

This disciple had the desire to go the whole way with Jesus, even unto death. And who was it? It was Thomas, the doubter. But do you remember what happened when Jesus appeared to him after the resurrection and offered that Thomas might touch His side? Thomas fell to his knees and said, "My Lord and my God!" He loved Jesus. This is the clue, this is the beginning of the death march— that we *love* Jesus so much that we want to go to our death in order that He might live within us.

Then Jesus himself takes us the next step: He says, "If any man love me, my Father will love him, and we will come and make our home with him." What's He talking about? This is part of His farewell speech in the fourteenth chapter of John. He's talking about the gift of the Holy Spirit.

There are depths to self, even when I am redeemed, that my feelings cannot touch, that my thoughts cannot reach, that my will power cannot move, *that nothing but the Holy Spirit of God through the Cross can touch and transform.* After we come in surrender to the foot of the Cross, only God's Holy Spirit can get down deep enough to really get at the roots of this self which stands in the way of God's power.

The Upper-Room Experience

For every Christian there must be "upper-room" moments, as there were with the apostles waiting for the initial outpouring of the Holy Spirit. They waited upon the Lord. They weren't ready to go out and carry on any work yet, because the Lord hadn't gotten down into these depths in their lives. There is a need for every Christian who wants to grow in Christ and become a power for Him to be open to upper-room experiences at times in his life.

Rees Howells, the great Welsh intercessor, tells of an upper-room experience in this way: "It never dawned on me that the Holy Ghost is a person exactly like the Savior. I had only thought of Him as an influence coming upon meetings. My meeting with the Holy Ghost was just as real as my meeting with the Savior, several years before. I saw Him as a person, apart from flesh and blood, and He said to me: 'As the Savior had a body, so I dwell in the cleansed temple of the believer. I am a person. I am God. I come to ask you to give your body to me that I may work through it. But it must belong to me without reserve, for two persons with different wills can never live in the same body. If I come, I come as God and you must go. I shall not mix myself with yourself.' It meant every bit of my fallen nature was to go to the cross, and He would bring in his own life and nature. I took five days to make the decision, days which were spent alone with God. Like Isaiah, I saw the holiness of God, and seeing Him I saw my own corrupt nature. It wasn't sin that I saw, but nature touched by the fall. I was corrupt to the core. I knew I had to be cleansed. I saw that there was as much difference between the Holy Ghost and myself as between light and darkness.

"Nothing is more real to me than the process that I went through for that whole week. The Holy Spirit went on dealing with me, exposing the root of my nature, which was self. Sin was canceled and it wasn't sin He was dealing with. It was self. That thing which came from the fall. He wasn't going to take any superficial surrender. He put His finger on each part of my self life and I had to decide in cold blood. Day by day the dealing went on. He was coming in as God, and I had lived as a man, and what is permissible to an ordinary man, He told me, will not be permissible to you.

"The Lord told me that He would take out of my nature all taste for money, and any ambition for the ownership of money. Then there was the fact that I would never have the right to a choice in making a home. Other things were dealt with, including ambition, and on the fifth day my reputation was touched. By Friday night each issue had been faced. I knew exactly what was offered. The choice between temporal and eternal gain. The Spirit summed up the issue for me: 'On no account will I allow you to cherish a single thought of self. And the life I will live in you will be 100% for others. You will never be able to save yourself any more than the Savior could when He was on the earth. Now are you willing?' I bowed my head and said, 'Lord, I am willing!' This experience was a crisis which was followed by the process of sanctification, during which the Holy Spirit on the basis of the initial surrender, step by step replaced the self nature with His own divine nature."

We need upper-room experiences. The Lord will deal with each one of us in a marvelously personal way. If there is anything that the Holy Spirit does *not* do, it is to stamp His products out on an assembly-line basis. Your experience will be unique.

The experience of being filled with the Spirit is followed by a process of being purged by the Spirit. I remember kneeling one day at my altar to pray. I was irked that day; I had been for the whole week. I needed more patience dealing with my family, my people. I was praying for the Spirit to give me patience, and I began to feel the burden lifting, began to feel that the Lord was going to answer my prayer.

I had no more than gotten up and turned around from the altar when into the back of the church walked a person who irritated me. The flesh in me almost said out loud, "O Lord, what does *she* have to come here for? She irritates the life out of me!" And the Lord said, "Well, Son, you asked for patience; here is a chance to try it out."

Patience doesn't come from a sweet feeling kneeling at the altar. The scripture says: *"Tribulation* works patience."* That's how the Lord does it.

He will put in your pathway opportunities, challenges, trials—in order that this process of purging the self can take place. Paul had to have his old nature nailed down with a thorn in the flesh in order that God's purging program could take place. It was part of the Holy Spirit's program to crucify Saul of Tarsus, inch-by-inch.

Some people say, "Oh, this is all so *negative*. We want to have positive, hopeful thoughts." Well, positive thinking is good, and so is *honest* thinking. The Holy Spirit's ministry of *power* is only as effective in you as His ministry of *purging.* Only to the extent that self is purged can the living God enter in and flow through you.

These are deep things, things that happen way down

where the Spirit lives—deeper than your thoughts, deeper than your emotions. How can we sum it up? Let us suggest a simple prayer pattern as you wake up in the morning. Before you get out of bed, open yourself to the complete program that the Holy Spirit has outlined for you. This is the way you're going to become a channel of His power—when He takes over, when this paradox that Paul so beautifully states for us begins to be lived out in your life, when you become weak and the power of God flows through you with great might. Think of yourself as beginning a new day with this prayer: *O Holy Spirit of the living God, by faith I acknowledge Thy presence within me now. In the very depths of my being—deeper than my thoughts, deeper than my feelings, deeper than my will, Thou dost dwell. I worship Thee, I adore Thee, I love Thee, I thank Thee that Thou dost deign to take up dwelling in my body, yea, to call it Thy very temple. Most of all I thank Thee that Thou hast revealed to me the Lord Jesus Christ, my Savior, and that Thou hast appropriated unto me all the benefits of His atoning death.*

And now this new day I offer myself completely and utterly to Thy plans and guidance. Lead me and prepare me toward any opportunity where thou wouldst have me experience a fresh infilling of Thy mighty power. And do Thou this day lay upon me my particular cross, my particular opportunity to die to self that Christ might live in me. O Holy Spirit, this day let self within me become weak unto death that Christ might live within me, that His power might manifest itself through me. Let me become a channel of love and healing, of power and blessing to everyone I meet. O Holy Spirit, to the end that our loving Father in heaven might be glorified and might find pleasure this day in me. Amen.

Chapter 13

The Government of God

*"About this time I realized that some of the Jews had
married women from Ashdod, Ammon, and Moab, and that
many of their children spoke in the language of Ashdod and
couldn't speak the language of Judah at all. So I argued
with these parents and cursed them and punched a few of
them and knocked them around and pulled out their hair"*
(Neh. 13:23-25, TLB).

Did Nehemiah live up to his name, "The Lord Is Comfort"? How many would feel "comforted" being dealt with
in this way?

One man's up-dated response to these verses was: "Who
does this Nehemiah think he is? He won't let us date those
cute girls on the other side of the wall. He doesn't own us!
This is our city and we'll do what we want to!"

Nehemiah was God's governor. The book that bears his
name teaches us some important truths about God's government. It is well to examine our attitude toward the government of God, for it was rebellion against the government
of God that caused Satan to be cast out of heaven, and it
was rebellion against the government of God that caused
Adam and Eve to be put out of the Garden of Eden. Restoration of the government of God was Christ's purpose for
coming down to earth. The very first words that He
preached, the first words of the gospel recorded in Mark
1:44 were, "The time is fulfilled and the kingdom of God is
at hand; repent and believe the gospel." The time has come

to restore the government of God; turn back from your rebellion and believe this good news!

The Gospel (Good News) of the Kingdom

Yes, the government of God is good news, because it signals an end to the disorder and misery brought on by rebellion against God. When we describe ourselves in some of the ancient liturgies of the church as "poor, miserable sinners," we're telling it like it really is. Satan may make it sound like fun, fun, fun, when he comes on with his commercials, but we all know from bitter experience that taking his bait spells miserable, miserable, miserable. Jesus comes preaching good news: the reign of sin is over, the government of God is at hand.

When the government of God begins to get a grip on your thoughts, you know that God has put you back on Square 1 again. You are looking for that which will bring glory to Christ, and which He alone can bring to pass.

It was Albert Schweitzer, the German theologian who later became a medical missionary to Africa, that startled the theological world several generations ago with his book, *The Quest of the Historical Jesus*. He pointed out that the central burden of Jesus' preaching and mission was to proclaim the Kingdom of God. Jesus' preaching about loving your neighbor, about truth and morality and justice—issues that the liberal theologians of the 19th century had majored on—were all secondary, according to Schweitzer. The thing Jesus was primarily concerned with was reestablishment of the government of God.

Schweitzer came to some very unorthodox and unacceptable conclusions; for instance, he said that Jesus expected God's government to be set up immediately, which didn't happen, and therefore Jesus was really mistaken. But Schweitzer nevertheless did the church a great service because his initial insight was correct: the burden of Jesus' heart, the burden of His preaching was *the government of God*.

When Christ healed the sick or cast out demons, it was to release people from the bondage of Satan's kingdom so they could be brought into God's kingdom. When He taught the crowds, He was instructing them in the way the government of God functions; e.g., the parables about the Kingdom describe how the government of God is established, how it functions. The Sermon on the Mount is basically a description of life under the government of God. His call to people was not a call to accept a teaching or philosophy of life; it was the call to "Follow me! Give up your loyalty to the kingdom of Satan and this world and commit yourself to me and my Father's kingdom!" When He went to the Cross, He entered into the battle which finally, once-and-for-all, would establish the supremacy of the government of God.

The apostle Paul recounts for us the result of that cosmic struggle in the first and second chapters of Colossians: "He has rescued us out of the darkness and gloom of Satan's kingdom and brought us into the kingdom of his dear Son, who bought our freedom with his blood and forgave us all our sins. . . . It was through what His Son did that God cleared a path for everything to come to him—all things in heaven and on earth—for Christ's death on the cross has made peace with God for all by his blood. This includes you who were once so far away from God. You were his enemies and hated him and were separated from him by your evil thoughts and actions, yet now he has brought you back as his friends. He has done this through the death on the cross of his own human body, and now as a result Christ has brought you into the very presence of God, and you are standing there before him with nothing left against you— nothing left that he would even chide you for; the only condition is that you fully believe the Truth, standing in it steadfast and firm, strong in the Lord, convinced of the Good News that Jesus died for you, and never shifting from trusting him to save you. This is the wonderful news that came to each of you, and is now spreading all over the world. . . . God took away Satan's power to accuse you of sin, and God openly displayed to the whole world Christ's triumph at the cross where your sins were all taken away" (1:13, 14, 20-23; 2:15, TLB).

The Good News is that the Lord Jesus Christ, the Commander-in-Chief of the armies of heaven, has reestablished the government of God and reestablished us as citizens of His kingdom!

Have you come into this Kingdom? Have you experienced the government in a personal way? Have you found it sometimes difficult to adjust to, or at other times elusive and hard to grasp? This is the point that led Albert Schweitzer astray: The government of God is not like the government of the United States or Russia—out in the open for all to see. And so some conclude that it is all a mistake or an illusion. But Jesus said, "My kingdom is not of this world." He did not say it was not *in* this world but it is not *of* this world. In other words, its authority and power do not depend upon any of the power structures of this world.

This is a decisive point for anyone who wants to live under the government of God. The government of God does not function in an open and obvious way; it operates only where people in faith accept its unseen presence and authority. Schweitzer said Jesus proclaimed the Kingdom of God, the Kingdom didn't come; therefore Jesus was wrong. But the Bible says that Jesus proclaimed the Kingdom, Jesus laid the foundation of the Kingdom through His victory on the Cross, and Jesus is bringing the Kingdom to reality in the way that the wisdom of God has decreed— first among a people who receive it by faith and only then openly in the sight of all, at the end of the age.

So we have the great privilege of ground-floor citizenship in the Kingdom of God. Even now, during the low-profile phase, we can experience the reality and blessing of God's government.

Government: A Vehicle for Love!

What is the government of God like? What happens

when it really begins to function? What difference does it make in our everyday life? One of the primary functions of government is to provide *stability*. Let me put it another way: Government insures that people will do certain things even when they may not feel like it. God's government protects us from the random choices and actions that individuals might take if they were simply left to follow the dictates of their own feelings or choices in every situation.

If we had a big community celebration with the slogan, "A Good Neighbor Is a Careful Driver," and got everybody enthused and involved, I can imagine people carefully driving down the street, the very embodiment of courtesy and consideration. We would not need a four-way stop at the corner—every driver would approach the intersection carefully, nod to drivers approaching on the cross street and alternate through the intersection in a totally courteous and orderly way. Under the inspiration of special occasions, people can be encouraged to act in a loving and considerate way.

But when Monday morning comes, and the main street is choked up with commuter traffic and the slogans and emphasis of the Good-Neighbor Weekend have grown a little faint, aren't you glad for the four-way stop? Because *you* may still be the soul of safe and considerate driving, but what about those fourteen bumper-to-bumper late-for-work commuters waiting to careen onto the main street?

We have learned in the family—and even more so when we go into extended household living—that enthusiasm, good intentions, yes, and Spirit-led dedication can carry the members along for a short while, but then one either comes to government or the household falls apart. It isn't merely that people cool in their love and consideration for each other. Without government their love lacks coordination.

Left to their own feelings or convenience, three people might all be moved to prepare supper the same evening, the next day all the cooks might be moved to take late afternoon naps. Or four people might suddenly jam the bathroom door at 7:00 a.m., intent on a leisurely bath, or wander in for household prayers anywhere between 5:30-8:30 in the morning. Left to how I *feel*, some mornings I wouldn't go to work, some days I'd skip meetings that I had planned, sometimes I'd make decisions without checking with other people who are involved. Government provides an orderly way for people to live together.

Nor does government need to be a cold, impersonal thing. Good government actually provides a reliable way for us to express our love for one another.

Ron Hals, a professor of Old Testament at Trinity Seminary in Columbus, Ohio, has written a book called, *The Place of the Law in the Old Testament*. He says that the law, which was essentially God's government among the people of Israel, was given to help the people express their love and thanks to God. God had rescued them out of slavery, was bringing them to the Promised Land, and the question naturally came up: How can we express our love and loyalty to such a God? God responded to that unspoken question by giving them the law, a God-revealed pattern for expressing love to God and to other people.

Jesus picks up on this same truth when He says, "If you love me, you will keep my commandments" (John 14:15). The government of God, which is expressed in His commandments, is not a heavy burden of "oughts." It is a God-revealed way for expressing love.

So when we talk about the government of God, we must not see it as something rigid and impersonal, standing in opposition to His love. Rather, it is His way of showing us how best to love Him and one another. "This is the love of God, that we keep his commandments. And his commandments are not burdensome" (1 John 5:3). The government of God is God's answer for those who say, "Lord, show us how to love you!"

Government: A Means of Protection

Another basic job of government is to *protect* its people.

The Constitution of the United States speaks, in the Preamble, about "insuring domestic tranquillity and providing for the common defense." Part of God's purpose in establishing government for His people is to protect them.

A particular danger that Nehemiah dealt with in the Old Testament was the danger of *subversion*. The government of God takes a bead on forces that would creep in to subvert His people and rob them of the peace and security which the Lord has won for them at great cost. Subversion is a particular concern of the government of God because it can creep up almost unnoticed and for that reason is particularly dangerous.

In the thirteenth chapter we see this Old Testament governor of God's people deal with subversion. He comes back to Jerusalem after an absence and finds that the faith and life of the people has been subverted in three particular ways. Nehemiah was a man uniquely led of God. The way he handles this situation can be instructive for us in similar circumstances.

1. *Unwholesome Relationships*

Most people can look back upon some close personal relationships which turned out to be a negative influence upon their lives. Something about a person was attractive to you, otherwise the relationship never would have started up in the first place. But little by little it began to feed things into your life that were unwholesome. You began to think differently, talk differently, act differently. Maybe you realized some of this was happening, but because you didn't feel up to breaking off the relationship, you overlooked or rationalized things that gnawed at your conscience. Little by little that unwholesome relationship caused you to compromise some of your basic attitudes and convictions.

Until we get into a situation like this, it's easy to overestimate our own moral strength. We think, "I know what I believe and stand for. No one is going to influence me if I don't want to be influenced." But close personal relationships generate the kind of heat and strength that can bend the strongest convictions. The wisest person in the world can be subverted by an unwholesome relationship. Nehemiah reminded the Israelites that even Solomon, whose wisdom was a legend in the whole world, drifted into sin because of the unwholesome influence of foreign women in his life and kingdom.

When Nehemiah returned to Jerusalem he found that a number of unwholesome relationships were subverting the people. Eliashib, the high priest, was "connected" to Tobiah, one of the men who had most strongly opposed the Jews when they were rebuilding the walls of Jerusalem. He had even let Tobiah take over one of the rooms in the temple for his personal quarters. One of Eliashib's grandsons had married a daughter of Sanballat, another enemy of the Jews. Many of the Jews, contrary to the clear word of God, had married women of Ashdod, Ammon, and Moab. Half of their children were growing up speaking these foreign tongues, strangers to the language and heritage of Israel.

Both Old and New Testaments warn God's people about the danger of unwholesome relationships. Proverbs 15:29 says, "Wickedness loves company—and leads others into sin." Ephesians 5:3-8 says, "But immorality and all impurity or covetousness must not even be named among you, as is fitting among saints. Let there be no filthiness, nor silly talk, nor levity, which are not fitting; but instead let there be thanksgiving. Be sure of this, that no immoral or impure man or one who is covetous (that is, one who is an idolater) has any inheritance in the kingdom of Christ and of God. Let no one deceive you with empty words, for it is because of these things that the wrath of God comes upon the sons of disobedience. *Therefore do not associate with them*, for once you were darkness, but now you are light in the Lord." In 2 Corinthians 6:14, the apostle specifically warns about the danger of entering into an unwholesome marriage relationship: "Do not be mismated with unbelievers. For what fellowship has light with darkness?"

When Nehemiah saw how unwholesome relationships had subverted the people, he dealt with the matter decisively. He tossed Tobiah's furniture out of the temple, gave orders for the rooms to be cleansed, and had the vessels of worship brought back and put in place. He met with families that had intermarried with foreigners: "I contended with them, and cursed them, and beat some of them and pulled out their hair; and I made them take an oath in the name of the Lord God, saying, 'You shall not give your daughters to their sons, or take their daughters for your sons or for yourselves.' "

Not very gentle treatment! Not very loving, some would say. But when we consider the government of God, we must let the Spirit cleanse our thinking of a short-sighted understanding of God's love. One person upon reading these verses observed, "God's primary interest was not the people's immediate comfort and well-being, but restoration of His people to His purpose." That's long-range love. That's love with fiber and backbone, willing to take a stand and do battle against that which would subvert the beloved and cause him to miss God's best. Don't let the world's sentimental and self-centered notion of love fog up the landscape of your understanding. Make no mistake about it: The government of God is an expression of His unwavering love.

2. Neglect of Tithes and Offerings

God had made ample provision for the spiritual care of His people: one whole tribe, roughly ten percent of the people of Israel, was set aside for priesthood and ministry. This tribe, the tribe of Levi, was not given land like the other tribes; they were to be supported by the tithes and offerings of the people so as to be free to carry on their ministry.

But the people became neglectful in their giving. The

Levites were forced to go out and work on farms to support themselves. The service and worship in the temple declined.

We aren't told precisely what lay behind this fall-off in giving. Perhaps it was plain old-fashioned selfishness, or it may have been thoughtless neglect. In any case, it was subverting God's people. It was robbing them of the kind of spiritual care and guidance that God wanted them to have.

Nehemiah restored the practice of tithing and brought the Levites back into their ministry. The government of God puts a high value on spiritual leadership. Not just big names like Moses, David, or in this time of restoration, Ezra and Nehemiah; or, in our day, a Billy Graham or Pope John Paul, but leadership that spreads out among the people and down to "thousands, hundreds, fifties, and tens." (See Exodus 18:21.) There need to be enough people set apart for ministry so that the rank and file of God's people can have close contact with them. They are not sheep without a shepherd. They are a flock well tended and cared for.

Tithes are not only important for the support of ministry; tithes are a visible acknowledgement of the government of God over one's material possessions. When I tithe I am saying, "Lord, all that I have comes from you and belongs to you. Accept these 'first fruits' as a sign that everything I have is at your disposal."

The government of God extends to our money, not for God's sake (He's solvent!) but for *our* sake. God has so arranged things in His Kingdom that material prosperity is linked to the practice of giving. "Give and it will be given unto you. . . . Sow bountifully and you will reap bountifully. . . . Bring the full tithes into the storehouse and thereby put me to the test if I will not open up the windows of heaven and pour down on you an overflowing blessing."

Withholding tithes and offerings subverts God's people because it allows the world to gain a foothold in their economic affairs, and thus over their whole life. When you put your economic affairs under the government of God through giving of tithes and offerings, you erect a powerful defense against enslavement by the world.

The world seeks to intimidate us by the threat of poverty. "Hang onto everything you get—bad times are coming. You won't have enough!" No matter how much we have, it's amazing how compelling that taunt is!

The believer who lives under the government of God knows the source of his security and supply. With the writer to Hebrews he can say, "Keep your life free from the love of money, and be content with what you have; for he has said, 'I will never leave you nor forsake you.' Hence we can confidently say, 'The Lord is my helper, I will not be afraid; what can man do to me?' " (Heb. 13:6).

3. Neglect of Worship

Nothing so set Israel apart from her neighbors as her observance of the Sabbath. So central was the Sabbath to the life of Israel that one writer has said, "It was not so much that Israel kept the Sabbath as that the Sabbath kept Israel!"

Under the incessant pressure of the world, human memory of God's will and God's ways grows short. We forget His faithfulness and provision in times past. We fall to doubting that He is truly with us, or that His Word is binding upon us, in the present situation.

I find this to be especially true, for instance in my prayer life. No matter how often I have experienced the blessedness of prayer-communion with my Lord, no matter how vivdly I have seen Him answer prayer before my eyes, the world-view sneaks in at the dawning of a new day and whispers, "Set your prayer time aside. I have more urgent matters for your attention." Subversion, at the very heart of the government of God! Subversion of our personal relationship with the King.

Nehemiah found the Sabbath observance of Israel in shambles. One person studying this chapter entitled it,

"God's Man Takes Charge!" And take charge he did: "What is this evil thing you are doing, profaning the Sabbath day? If you do so again I will lay hands upon you!"

God's people need to be shaken up when they have been subverted by the world into a lackadaisical attitude toward worship and toward their personal communion with God. No personal relationship, human or divine, can be sustained on memory alone. It must be continually refreshed—daily prayer, regular coming together with fellow believers for worship and mutual encouragement.

One of the great deceptions that has subverted God's people is what I would call an intellectual notion of "faith," which thinks that if I know something about God I "have" it. If I know in my head that God forgives sin, I am forgiven; if I know in my head that God gives the Holy Spirit, I have the Holy Spirit; if I know in my head that Christ promises victory over the world, then I have that victory. Not so! When the world subverts God's people, they lose the protection and blessing of God's government.

The government of God is not an empty phrase. It is a reality. Where it is subverted, we become subject to other governing powers and the government of God is thwarted among us.

One man commented on this thirteenth chapter of Nehemiah, "God's people need parenting, parenting, parenting!" To counter that which would subvert His people, God gives us governors, those who will love us enough to insist that we come back under the government of God from which we have strayed.

It is easy to take offense at a governor, to see him simply as a person who is shaking you up rather than as a messenger of God. There is a sad history both in the Old and New Testaments of God's people rejecting those whom God sent to establish His government. In an anguish of rejected love Jesus cried out, "O Jerusalem, Jerusalem, killing the prophets and stoning those who are sent to you! How often would I have gathered your children together as a hen gathers her brood under her wings, and you would not! Behold, your house is forsaken. And I tell you, you will not see me until you say, 'Blessed is he who comes in the name of the Lord!' " (Luke 13:34-35). Our vision of Christ, our fellowship with Him, depends upon the way we receive those whom He sends to govern us.

Lord, do not abandon us to the government of this world and of the prince of this world. Forgive us where we have allowed ourselves to become subverted. Send us your modern-day Nehemiahs. Give us eyes to see and hearts to heed those whom you send to establish your blessed government among us!